"If you want to better understand the Bible—a library of sixty-six books written by dozens of authors over hundreds and hundreds of years—then *The 30-Minute Bible* by Craig G. Bartholomew and Paige P. Vanosky ... book you need. They clearly and succinctly present the overarching the ... ithin the Bible's pages by helping you understand the ebb and fl ... ou will come away from reading with a greater underst ... or this all-time classic."

Michael Buckner Fanning, pastor at Th ... ident of MBF Enterprises

"The Bible can be a daunting ... ty, and journey through thousands of years make compl ... a daunting task for even the most dedicated of readers. *The 30-M* ... akes the fear out of even opening to the first page. One of the gifts of read ... ipture is discovering how relational God is. The approachable nature of this book reflects God's desire to relate to us through God's Word even today. To be able to spend thirty minutes a day to hear God's eternal voice in our world is nothing short of a gift."

Margaret Grun Kibben, chaplain, US House of Representatives

"It is impossible to live well, to be a self, without knowing the story we inhabit. For followers of Jesus, that story comes from the Bible. Whether you are new to the Bible or looking for a fresh engagement with it, *The 30-Minute Bible* is a version I highly recommend. Use it and you move from simply knowing verses to seeing the Bible bursting with a story—and an invitation for you to make meaning of your life via that story."

Todd Hunter, Anglican bishop and author of *Christianity Beyond Belief*

"Bible teacher Paige Vanosky and noted Bible scholar Craig Bartholomew have given us a labor of love born out of their lives committed to teaching, sharing, living out, and wrestling with the Bible. . . . Their gift to any first-time or veteran student of the Bible is extending God's own invitation to every person of any age, background, and context to walk into the world of the Scriptures, encounter the living God, and engage in a lifelong apprenticeship that begins with a thirty-minute introduction but which lasts into eternal life."

Neal D. Presa, Village Community Presbyterian Church, Rancho Santa Fe, California

"The authors have given us solid biblical knowledge from a broadly ecumenical point of view that teachers from any Christian tradition can use with confidence. This book is for people who very much want to take God seriously and find a pathway to greater understanding of God's Word so that they can better follow Jesus. This book is for those who are convinced that God actually does communicate to real people in the context of their real lives. It will be a worthy resource for teachers and for groups wanting to get a sense of the big picture."

Jack W. Baca, senior pastor of the Village Community Presbyterian Church, Rancho Santa Fe, California

"Bartholomew's scholarly expertise and Vanosky's expertise teaching the Bible to everyday people from diverse backgrounds pair nicely in this helpful resource that captures the story line of the Bible in six acts (and thirty short chapters), emphasizing God's kingship. Readers who are new to the Bible or are unsure of how it fits together will enjoy this book."

Kevin S. Chen, associate professor of Old Testament, Christian Witness Theological Seminary

"The Bible is an extremely complex book made up of many books written in a variety of literary genres over a long period of time. It is easy to get lost amid this complexity. And so it is part of our missional and theological task today to provide clear maps that tell the story as lucidly as possible to enable God's people to place different parts of the Bible within its overarching narrative structure. In *The 30-Minute Bible* Bartholomew and Vanosky provide just such a map. It can help even beginners to not just understand the Bible's story but be shaped by it instead of the false, idolatrous stories of our culture."

Michael W. Goheen, professor of missional theology at Covenant Seminary, St. Louis, and director of theological education at the Missional Training Center, Phoenix

"There can be no more urgent task for the church today than to recover the biblical story. Here in thirty accessible, informative, and satisfying bites, Bartholomew and Vanosky clearly set out the key developments in the biblical story from creation to new creation. This book will enable the reader to see how the Bible fits together, to identify the big themes, and to recognize how Jesus fulfils God's purposes for humankind and for the world. And, crucially, it will also enable readers to find their own place in the unfolding drama of God's great story. As a pastor, this is the book I have been waiting for! I want to put a copy into the hands of every family under my care."

William Olhausen, rector of St. Matthias Church, Dublin, Ireland

THE 30-MINUTE BIBLE

GOD'S STORY FOR EVERYONE

CRAIG G. BARTHOLOMEW AND PAIGE P. VANOSKY

An imprint of InterVarsity Press
Downers Grove, Illinois

InterVarsity Press
P.O. Box 1400, Downers Grove, IL 60515-1426
ivpress.com
email@ivpress.com

InterVarsity Press® is the book-publishing division of InterVarsity Christian Fellowship/USA®, a movement of students and faculty active on campus at hundreds of universities, colleges, and schools of nursing in the United States of America, and a member movement of the International Fellowship of Evangelical Students. For information about local and regional activities, visit intervarsity.org.

All Scripture quotations, unless otherwise indicated, are taken from The Holy Bible, New International Version®, NIV®. Copyright © 1973, 1978, 1984, 2011 by Biblica, Inc.™ Used by permission of Zondervan. All rights reserved worldwide. www.zondervan.com. The "NIV" and "New International Version" are trademarks registered in the United States Patent and Trademark Office by Biblica, Inc.™

The publisher cannot verify the accuracy or functionality of website URLs used in this book beyond the date of publication.

Interior black and white illustrations by Martin Erspamer OSB

Tabernacle illustration is ©2019 InterVarsity Press. First published in The Old Testament in Seven Sentences *by Christopher J. H. Wright.*

Cover design and image composite: Chris Tobias
Interior design: Jeanna Wiggins
Cover image: Christ and the Eucharist (illustration): permission to use image given by Brother Erspamer

ISBN 978-0-8308-4784-6 (print)
ISBN 978-0-8308-4785-3 (digital)

Printed in the United States of America ∞

InterVarsity Press is committed to ecological stewardship and to the conservation of natural resources in all our operations. This book was printed using sustainably sourced paper.

Library of Congress Cataloging-in-Publication Data
A catalog record for this book is available from the Library of Congress.

P	20	19	18	17	16	15	14	13	12	11	10	9	8	7	6	5	4	3	2	1
Y	38	37	36	35	34	33	32	31	30	29	28	27	26	25	24	23	22	21

CONTENTS

ACT FIVE
Spreading the News of the King:
The Mission of the Church

ACT SIX
The Return of the King:
Redemption Completed

PREFACE

ONE MIGHT WONDER how two very different people from two different continents came together to write this book—Craig, a noted biblical scholar based in Cambridge, UK, and me (Paige), a less well-known Bible teacher living in San Diego.

It began with a question: "Thirty minutes? Can I really summarize the entire Bible in just thirty minutes?" I wasn't sure I knew the answer, but I had just joined a book club and needed to review a book—but what book? Truth be told, I had joined the group in part because I wanted to hear about the books I did not have time to read. I have always loved reading, but for some years I had found myself without time to do much of that type of reading. So I sent out a call for suggestions.

I was shocked when a few people suggested I review the Bible. Granted, for many years I had been leading a chronological overview of the Bible to a rather ecumenical group of women—Catholic, Protestant, skeptic, strong believers, and Jewish Christians. The discussion from this mixed group made for great insight into differing views and for much personal reflection. I could see this background would be helpful for speaking to a larger group of women with beliefs unknown to me. But could I possibly explain the story of the Bible in just thirty minutes? So with the valuable assistance of my Bible study group, I put together a thirty-minute talk. And as friends began asking for copies, the idea of *The 30-Minute Bible* was born.

One slight problem was in the way—I had never been to seminary, and I was not at all comfortable releasing such an important book without scholarly assistance. It would be years before I discovered Craig Bartholomew. Craig is a highly regarded biblical scholar and the author of numerous scholarly books covering a wide range of topics. He is deeply interested in opening the story of the Bible up to the layperson. His unique scholarly insight and intriguing perspective on the story found within the Bible are immensely valuable to understanding this otherwise complex story. It has been a privilege to work with him as together we have sought to distill the long and meandering story of the Bible into one we hope you will find easily read and understood.

INTRODUCTION

How *You* Can Read and Understand the Bible

THE BIBLE REMAINS the bestselling book of all time. You may well have one hidden away somewhere in your house yourself. But while the Bible continues to sell incredibly well, it is often not read.

In many cases, this is not for lack of trying. Begin at the beginning—which sounds perfectly logical—and you may soon become bogged down in the laws of Exodus and Leviticus, the second and third books of the Bible, wondering what on earth they have to do with your life today. And so the Bible returns to its shelf, leaving you discouraged and feeling like you could never understand this strange book, as much as you would like to.

Why then read the Bible? To some the Bible is the basis for the largest religion in the world, Christianity, while for others it has been so influential historically that we need to be aware of it as literature if we are to understand our history. Still others seek to understand God and his relationship to the world. They wonder if God could possibly know or care about what is happening on earth and in our lives. To still others it is the book they meditate on to be instructed by and addressed by God, who has revealed himself particularly in Jesus Christ.

There are many good reasons for reading the Bible, and whatever your reason, the crucial question is *how* to go about reading it so that you can understand it. For many people, the experience of reading the Bible is like trying to force a big, bolted door open, and the million-dollar question is whether there's any key that can unlock the door and enable ordinary people like us to read and understand it.

The really good news of this book is that there is indeed such a key! We have found this key to work through years of teaching the Bible in home, church, and university settings. We have experienced again and again that this key really works. What, then, is this key?

Craig has a terrible sense of direction and can easily get lost. Thus, he is constantly grateful for GPS, with a voice telling him where to turn, which exit to take on the many roundabouts, etc., as he drives between his home in the town of March and Cambridge, UK, where he works. For navigating unknown roads, GPS is indispensable. But imagine if he is planning a lecture tour in America, a tour that includes speaking in several major cities. What would he need to plan his trip? The best tool to get him started is not GPS but a large-scale map so that he can connect the dots between all the different places he needs to visit. Then he can see how his tour fits together as a whole. Only after that can he attend to the details.

OLD TESTAMENT		NEW TESTAMENT	
THE PENTATEUCH	**THE PROPHETS**	**THE GOSPELS**	**THE LETTERS**
Genesis	*Major Prophets*	(The Life of Christ)	*From Paul*
Exodus	Isaiah	Matthew	Romans
Leviticus	Jeremiah	Mark	1 & 2 Corinthians
Numbers	(Lamentations)	Luke	Galatians
Deuteronomy	Ezekiel	John	Ephesians
	Daniel		Philippians
THE HISTORY			Colossians
Joshua	*Minor Prophets*	**ACTS**	1 & 2 Thessalonians
Judges	Hosea	(The Activities	1 & 2 Timothy
Ruth	Joel	of the Apostles)	Titus
1 & 2 Samuel	Amos		Philemon
1 & 2 Kings	Obadiah		
1 & 2 Chronicles	Jonah		*From Others*
Ezra	Micah		Hebrews
Nehemiah	Nahum		James
Esther	Habakkuk		1 & 2 Peter
	Zephaniah		1, 2, & 3 John
POETRY & WISDOM	Haggai		Jude
Job	Zechariah		
Psalms	Malachi		**REVELATION**
Proverbs			(A book of
Ecclesiastes			apocalyptic writing)
Song of Solomon			

Figure 1.1. The books and collections of the Bible

The same is true with the Bible. No matter how enthusiastic you may be to get into the Bible, it's easy to get lost in the myriad details. For example, look at the contents page of any Bible—we suggest you use one in a modern translation[1]—or look through the contents page above and you will see straightaway that the Bible consists not of one book but of dozens of books! And, as you will see from the contents page, there are two major parts to the Bible: the Old Testament and the New Testament, which is like the distinction between the southern and the northern hemispheres on a map of the world.[2]

Right away we see from this table of contents that the Bible is broken into two parts—the Old and New Testaments, delineating the time before Christ and after Christ, respectively. The books in each of these two testaments take us on a chronological journey through time, from the creation of the world as told in Genesis to the prophesied end as told in Revelation. As if this were not confusing enough, browse through the headings of sections and you may come across strange words like "The Pentateuch," "Gospels," "Acts," and "Revelation," and you will also notice soon enough that there are different types of literature in the Bible: history, poetry, wisdom (what is "wisdom"?), and, in the New Testament, many letters (or "epistles").

As helpful as the headings are in the Bible's table of contents, they add confusion for a new reader and certainly do not provide us with the sort of large-scale map we need to understand the Bible. In our experience, even when familiar with a good number of Bible stories, many people don't know how they fit together. Imagine having pieces of a jigsaw puzzle without the picture to guide you as you assemble them! Likewise, we need a big picture or a large-scale map to guide our reading of the Bible so that we can see how the pieces fit together.

Now, crucially, if a map of America is to help Craig plan his tour, it has to be accurate. It must fit with what is on the ground. And so it is with a large-scale map of the Bible; it must fit with the nature of the Bible. And what is the nature of the Bible? The overarching shape of the Bible is that of a grand, sprawling story. That's right: *story*. This gets us close to the key that unlocks the Bible.

We humans resonate deeply with stories. If you want to get to know someone, sooner or later you find yourself saying, "Tell me about yourself!"—or, in other words, "Tell me your story." "Where were you born, what school did you go to, what is your family like, what do you do, etc., etc.?" To a greater extent than we may realize, we make sense of our own lives and enter into the lives of others through stories.

The key to understanding the Bible is to see that *it tells a story of the whole world*, beginning with the creation of the world and ending with the wrapping up of history. Its plot unfolds between these two bookends with Jesus at the heart of it all. Getting to know the story of the Bible enables us to read it while seeing how the many pieces fit into an overarching whole.

We probably all know that Jesus is central to the Bible. We can easily miss, however, that to understand Jesus, who we learn about mainly in the New Testament, we need to go all the way back to Adam and Eve and then trace the story forward to see how Jesus fits into it and fulfills it. The story of the Bible is the large-scale map that enables us to see how it all fits together.

The good news is that this small book is designed precisely to provide you with just such a large-scale map and with other cultural and historical information that will deepen your understanding of the Bible's story. This overview can help you read the Bible with understanding and an awareness of how individual parts fit into the big picture. Paige has been teaching the content of this book to Christians and non-Christians for twelve years, and the result has been transformative. The same can happen to you.

The 30-Minute Bible leads you through the major landmarks of the storyline of the Bible. We want to take you on the journey from the beginning of the world to its end, with the amazing story in between. The book is arranged in bite-sized chunks so that if you set aside thirty minutes each day for thirty days, you'll become familiar with the entire story. At each stage we suggest readings from the Bible—as you read them, we think you'll find that yes, you *can* understand the Bible. Do get hold of a Bible in modern English. Many are available. For example, in this book when we quote from the Bible, we are using the New International Version (NIV), a very accessible version.

The Bible is a bottomless well that we can continue to study—and gain fresh insights from—our whole life long. At the same time, its overarching story can be grasped quickly. Indeed, a good test of this book having achieved its goal is that by the end, you should be able to tell the story of the Bible in about thirty minutes.

We're aware that you cannot engage with the Bible without having questions, just like the Bible study group Paige has been teaching for twelve years. These are important! We encourage you to keep a list of your questions and to seek answers to them, whether individually or in a group.

The British writer Margaret Silf tells the story of a luncheon at which each guest had brought a dish to share. She noted with sadness that a lovely rice salad was left untouched. And then she saw why this was the case: no spoon had been provided! A great feast awaits in the Bible, and we hope that this book will provide you with a spoon so that you can start eating!

Even as you plunge into the extraordinary story of the Bible, we want to provide you with two overarching frameworks that will be a great help to you as you navigate the sprawling story of the Bible. The Bible is a story, but it is a sprawling, detailed one with many, many smaller stories, plots, and twists and turns.

The first framework is this: imagine the whole biblical story as a *drama in six acts*.[3] As we tell the story, we will situate the different parts within these six acts:

✳ Act One. God Establishes His Kingdom: Creation

The story of the Bible begins with God as the great King creating everything from nothing and pronouncing it "very good" (chapters two and three).

✳ Act Two. Rebellion in the Kingdom: The Fall

Answers the question "What is wrong with our world?" It diagnoses our condition in relation to the rebellion of the first couple, Adam and Eve, and our own rebellion against God (chapter four).

✳ Act Three. The King Chooses Israel: Salvation Initiated

Is all about God's response to our rebellion. God chooses and forms a people, Israel, and lives among them. Israel is intended to live under God's reign and to show to the world what life is meant to be (chapters five through nineteen).

✳ Act Four. The Coming of the King: Salvation Accomplished

God's life with Israel climaxes in the coming of Jesus, the Savior of the world. Jesus lives the perfect life, dies by crucifixion, and then is raised from the dead. He ascends to the Father in heaven (chapters twenty through twenty-six).

✳ Act Five. Spreading the News of the King: The Mission of the Church

Begins with the pouring out of the Holy Spirit. The Spirit empowers the followers of Jesus to spread the good news of all that God has done in him. Many are converted and the church grows and spreads. Act five is the part of the drama in which we live (chapters twenty-seven through twenty-nine).

✳ Act Six. The Return of the King: Redemption Completed

Looks forward to the time when Jesus will come again in glory, bringing history to an end, ushering in the new heaven and earth, and establishing God's rule over everything (chapter thirty).

As you'll see, once we plunge into the story of the Bible, God is the central character, and he is consistently portrayed as the great King. Psalm 99:1 (NLT), for example, begins, "The LORD is king!" If you look at our six acts above, you will see that God's kingship or rule is the golden thread that holds the whole of the Bible together. Of course, unlike far too many kings in history, God rules, as we will see, with our best interests and those of his creation at heart.

The first three acts cover the Old Testament, the last three the New Testament. We will alert you throughout to which act you are in. We recommend that you memorize these six acts, even if you don't fully understand them at present. We will explain them as we go along but memorizing them now will provide you with useful hooks to hang the developing story on so that you'll be able to remember it.

The second framework is a timeline. Just as the six acts will keep you oriented on our journey, so too will the timeline. Much of the Bible is about God acting in history, and as you move through the story of the Bible, you'll find it helpful to refer back to the timeline to see just where you are in the great story of the Bible. The Bible is made up of two major parts, the Old Testament and the New Testament. As you can see, the Old Testament covers the story from the creation of the world to the time before Jesus. The New Testament tells the story of Jesus and all that happened as a result.

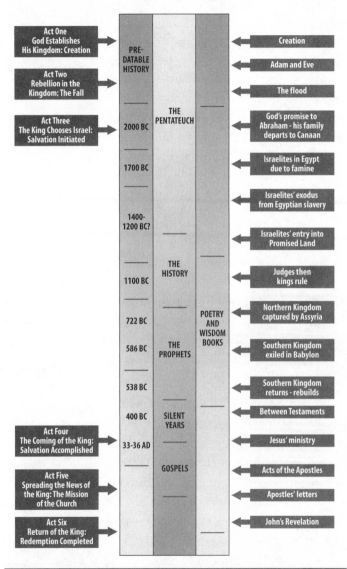

Act One
God Establishes His Kingdom: Creation

Act Two
Rebellion in the Kingdom: The Fall

Act Three
The King Chooses Israel: Salvation Initiated

Act Four
The Coming of the King: Salvation Accomplished

Act Five
Spreading the News of the King: The Mission of the Church

Act Six
Return of the King: Redemption Completed

PRE-DATABLE HISTORY

2000 BC

1700 BC

1400-1200 BC?

1100 BC

722 BC

586 BC

538 BC

400 BC

33-36 AD

THE PENTATEUCH

THE HISTORY

THE PROPHETS

SILENT YEARS

GOSPELS

POETRY AND WISDOM BOOKS

Creation

Adam and Eve

The flood

God's promise to Abraham - his family departs to Canaan

Israelites in Egypt due to famine

Israelites' exodus from Egyptian slavery

Israelites' entry into Promised Land

Judges then kings rule

Northern Kingdom captured by Assyria

Southern Kingdom exiled in Babylon

Southern Kingdom returns - rebuilds

Between Testaments

Jesus' ministry

Acts of the Apostles

Apostles' letters

John's Revelation

Figure 1.2. Bible history timeline

CREATION

ONCE I (PAIGE) WAS DRIVING through a particularly beautiful mountain range, enjoying the majestic scenery and listening to one of my favorite singers, Louis Armstrong. He was singing, "I see trees so green, red roses too, I see them bloom for me and you." Just as I crested the mountaintop and was able to see a vista of extraordinary beauty stretching to the horizons, the chorus of the song came on, "And I think to myself, 'What a wonderful world.'" It was a showstopping moment. Perhaps you have had a similar experience while watching a majestic sunrise or sunset in a magical setting, or when you've found yourself surrounded by the awakening beauty of spring. It is hard to experience such beauty and not reflect on where it has come from.

The Bible's answer is found in Genesis 1—it all comes from God, the Creator. Of course, in our modern world people have many questions about this, questions like, Can we really still believe in God as Creator today? How does creation relate to science and evolution? These are important questions, but it is just as important to remember that the authors of the Bible were not thinking about such questions as they wrote. Therefore, when it comes to creation we need first to listen to the Bible on its own terms before asking how its message relates to our questions today.

The biblical story takes us way back through the mists of time to "in the beginning." The cosmos and our world have not always existed; there was a "beginning" when the entire cosmos was brought into existence or created by God. It is appropriate, then, that the Bible, the story of our world, begins with these words: "In the beginning God created the heavens and the earth."

"The heavens and the earth" is a way of saying "absolutely everything!" If, for example, you wanted to refer to the whole of a person, you might say, "She is wonderful from the tips of her toes to the hair on her head," meaning that you love everything about her. The opening verse of the Bible does the same thing: from the earth all the way to the heavens, *every single thing* is made by God.

It is worth pausing to let the enormity of this sink in. Craig grew up in South Africa, and when he returns to his homeland, it is not uncommon to find stickers on items saying, "Made in South Africa." So too, in America we find stickers saying, "Made in America." From the Bible's perspective, every single thing in creation would have to have a sticker on it saying, "Made by God": kingfishers and worms, rainbows and sunsets, individuals and nations, human capacities to think, run, jump, dance, enjoy sex, and more. For those who sometimes think that faith in God is just about being spiritual and has little to do with the

material aspects of our world, we see in the very first chapter in the Bible that nothing could be further from the truth.

Genesis 1 tells about God's creation of light and time, of the sky, the oceans, and the earth. God sets up the sun and the moon and the stars in the sky, thereby introducing seasons into our life on earth. Once the three major places on earth are established—the earth, the sky, the seas—God provides inhabitants for each of them: sea creatures for the oceans; birds for the sky; and plants, animals, and humans for the land. At every point of his creative work God contemplates it and declares it "good," and when he has finished creating the world, he declares it "very good." It is an astonishing vision of all of life—with all its diversity and wonder—as God's creation.

The poet Gerard Manley Hopkins speaks of the world as "charged with the grandeur of God," an expression that captures what it means for the world to be "very good." Through television programs like *Blue Planet*, we are becoming aware of the immense variety of sea creatures, all made by God. For those of us who are gardeners or farmers, the wonderful variety of plants and flowers comes from God. For those of us who enjoy gazing at the stars and the planets, all are from God. The

Bible opens with the whole of the world in view and declares that it all originates from God.

If, like us, you love art, Genesis 1 is like being taken to the most extraordinary exhibition you have ever seen. But imagine if, even as you are exploring the exhibition with wide eyes, a friend comes up to you and asks, "Would you like to meet the artist?" Of course, your answer would be, "Yes." This is exactly what the Bible does in its opening chapters. Yes, the creation is wonderful, but even more wonderful is the One who made it, and a major aim of the Bible is to introduce us to the Creator God. What is the Creator like? The opening words begin to provide our answer.

As the Creator, God is, first, royalty par excellence. He is the great King. In the world in which the Old Testament—the first part of the Bible—was written, kings were often thought of as gods and wielded great power. But God's kingship exceeds all earthly kings. A king's word might be a command, but God simply says, "Let there be . . ." and that part of creation is ushered into existence. God is all powerful.

Second, some people have a spaceman view of God—he is there but distant and uninvolved in our world. On the contrary, this chapter reveals a God who speaks and sees and ponders his handiwork. Like any good craftsperson, he is deeply interested in what he has made.

Third, God is one; he is the one and only God. In the world in which the Old Testament was written, the nations believed in thousands of different gods, and they had all sorts of stories about them and temples for their worship. The early readers of Genesis 1 would have noticed that when two of these "gods," the sun and the moon, are created (see Genesis 1:14-19), the Bible deliberately avoids using the words "sun" and "moon," referring to them instead as "the greater light" (the sun) and "the lesser light" (the moon). Why? To make it quite clear that they are not gods but part of God's creation with a specific function in his universe. God is the one and only God.

Fourth, God is wonderfully loving and kind. A common view among the ancient nations was that the gods created humans because they were tired of doing all the chores and work, and thus they made humans to serve them as slaves so they could relax and party. In this view the gods are all too human: selfish, lazy, and self-serving, with no real interest in the humans they created. God is completely and gloriously different. He sets up the created world as the ideal home for humankind, as the place in which we can flourish and become fully and wonderfully human, as we will see in the next chapter.

Having listened to the opening story of the Bible on its own terms, we can see that many of us make the mistake of reading the opening chapters of the Bible with our twenty-first-century questions about science and evolution front and center. These are important questions, but we first need to listen to the powerful message of these chapters before engaging such questions. Although we cannot answer these questions fully here, do note that the opening chapters of the Bible tell us mainly about *who* created the world rather than *how* he created it. Rightly understood, there is no conflict between the best science and the Bible. Indeed, the view of the world as creation, and thus as ordered and capable of being known, motivated scientific study—and continues to motivate it, albeit often unconsciously. As the great twentieth-century Christian writer C. S. Lewis pointed out, "Men became scientific because they expected Law in

Nature, and they expected Law in Nature because they believed in a Legislator."[1] Science looks for order in the creation, and it can only be found because God put it there and created us with minds fitted to explore and discover God's ways with his world.

We cannot understand the rest of the Bible if we do not grasp creation. Just as the opening act in a drama sets the stage for all that is to come, so everything that follows stems from creation and takes place within creation. Creation sets the scene for all that will unfold in the rest of the Bible.

A part of God's creation is humanity, and we are surprised to read his declaration of humanity as "very good." But we know humanity is not very good. What happened, where did it go wrong, and does God care? Is he doing anything about it? This is the storyline we will follow throughout the rest of this book, a storyline that takes a dramatic turn in chapter four. But first we need to understand what God intended for humankind in the first place. That we find in the next chapter.

READING: Genesis 1:1–2:3

ADAM AND EVE

Why Are We Here?

HAVE YOU EVER BEGUN reading a book only to find you need to go back to the opening chapter again to understand what's happening later on? We have, and for good reason. The opening scene, the opening words, provide important clues for understanding what is to come. The same is true of the Bible. We will not understand the rest of the biblical story if we do not grasp the initial story of creation. Everything that follows stems from it, setting the scene for all that will unfold.

The same is true in our own lives. It helps to know where we come from so that we can understand who we are and why we respond as we do. It's no wonder, then, that if you ask almost anyone to name their biggest life questions, you will likely hear something like, "Why am I here? Why does the world exist? What is its origin? Do humans matter? If there is a God, is he involved or concerned with what goes on?" These and so many other questions have been asked by humans down through the ages. In fact, we see this question posed in the hymnbook of the Old Testament, the Psalms. Psalm 8 begins by reflecting on God's greatness as the Creator and then poses this question:

When I consider your heavens,
the work of your fingers,
the moon and the stars,
which you have set in place,
what is mankind that you are mindful of them,
human beings that you care for them? (Psalm 8:3-4)

"What are human beings? And does God really care about us?" We struggle with these questions most intensely when a crisis strikes, but the answers often seem so elusive. The biblical story provides us with vital and thought-provoking answers to these questions.

In the biblical story, we find that humans share a lot in common with animals, but we also find that they are very different. Only of humans is it said that they were created *in God's image*, in his likeness (Genesis 1:26-28). This is, in fact, a high point of the opening story of the Bible, but what does it mean? If you think about how great God is, this is an astonishing thing to say about humans. Imagine if we met your mother or your daughter and said to you, "Oh, she is your spitting image!" You might not like it, but you would know exactly what we meant.

In the same way, being made in God's image means that in some fundamental way we are *like* God. But how exactly? After all, there are so many ways in which we are not like God. Humans, for example, can only be in one place at one time, whereas God can be everywhere.

In the last chapter we noted that Genesis introduces God to us as the great King. Well, Genesis 1 tells us God created humanity in his image to be his royal stewards, placed in his creation to rule over it, care for it, and develop all the potential God has placed in it. By *rule*, the Bible does not mean exploit for our own purposes. Just as God is wonderfully other-person centered in creating an ideal home for us, so we are to live under his rule and to be *like him* in the exercise of our human rule, caring for creation and developing its potential so that God's glory is ever more clearly seen in his good creation.

Of course, to care for God's creation, we need to be a particular type of being; that is, being made in God's image also means that we are persons like God. Unlike animals, we can speak, think, and enter consciously into deep relationships in ways that animals cannot. Indeed, *conscious* relationality is at the core of what it means to be human, and in Genesis 2 and 3 the different relations that constitute humans come into focus.

The whole world is created as the ideal home for humans, but we cannot live everywhere, and so, after God creates the first couple, Adam and Eve, he establishes them in a particular place—namely, the Garden of Eden, meaning "delight." This magnificent home is also a place for them to work and develop. Adam and Eve have bodies and are related to the particular part of the world they inhabit. As bodies they need to eat to live, and the great park of Eden contains all the fruits and vegetables they will need to cultivate and to enjoy.

The first couple are farmers and park wardens of Eden, reminding us that part of being human is working, whether as a farmer, carpenter, businessperson, homemaker, etc. In our modern world many of us experience work as dreary and oppressive, and we will come to the reasons for that, but this should not detract from the fact that part of being human is to work.

Being human also means being male or female (Genesis 1:27); both men and women are created in the image of God. In Genesis 2 we read that none of the animals could fulfill Adam's need for companionship, so God created Eve, leading Adam to respond with a poem of joy and gratitude (Genesis 2:23). Man and woman are designed to complement each other

and the first couple does precisely that. Here we see the gift of marriage as a major way in which humans are intended to experience intimacy and companionship. Of course, not all of us are married. Paige is married to Bob. Craig is not married. But all of us need relationships with other humans to be human, whether those of marriage, family, or friends. We are made to love and to be loved, and as we are loved and love, we become fully alive.

But we aren't only made for relationship with the world and with one another—most importantly, we're made for relationship with God. We noted in our previous chapter that God is not a spaceman God, far off and distant. We learn that having placed Adam and Eve in Eden, God used to come and walk in the park, conversing with Adam and Eve. We can only imagine their conversations and deep fellowship

(Genesis 3:8). God is not far off. He made us for himself. Even as we live, work, and relate to one another, God wants to be deeply involved with us.

A helpful way to depict God's creation of humans as relational beings through and through is figure 3.1.

This diagram illustrates the four major relationships involved in our humanity. We are made above all else for a deep, personal relationship with God. Part of being in God's image is that we are conscious of ourselves; that is the relationship on the left-hand side, our relationship with ourselves. Some of us, for example, spend a long time making ourselves presentable before we go out shopping or to meet friends

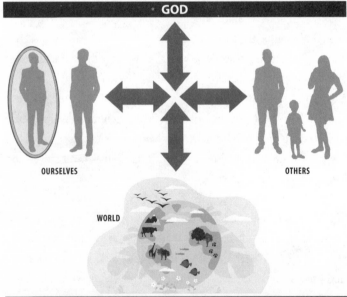

Figure 3.1. The four relationships

because we are conscious of how we look and how we appear to our fellow humans. We are meant to have a healthy view of ourselves; indeed, without one we cannot relate well to others. We are God's special creatures, but we are not God. As we have seen, we are not made to be isolated but are designed for deep relationships with others, the right-hand side. Finally, as humans we relate to the world and serve God by working in it and developing its potential so that God's glory is more and more visible in his handiwork.

We subtitled this chapter "Why Are We Here?" We are here because God put us here as his image bearers. We are made to love deeply and to be loved deeply. All four relationships that make up our humanity are meant to operate in harmony with one another. This exhilarating picture answers the question, What are human beings and why are we here?

Why then, does our experience too often feel far removed from this wonderful picture? What has gone wrong? We turn to that topic in the next chapter.

READINGS: Psalm 8 and Genesis 2:4-25

REBELLION IN EDEN

I N THE PREVIOUS CHAPTER we saw that God made us for relationship with himself, with one another, with ourselves, and with his world. Because we are wired for relationship, our relationships are where we most sense that all is not well. We all long to love others deeply and to be loved deeply in return, but time and again we are disappointed. And if you look at the earth and what we're doing to it, it's impossible not to see that something has gone terribly wrong.

Take one example: plastic. We use plastic for so many things, and each of our households churns out huge amounts of used plastic on a weekly basis. Through films like David Attenborough's *Blue Planet*, we can see what our use of plastic is doing to our oceans and to the sea creatures that inhabit them, as well as to the food chain. It's horrific to see turtles and other sea creatures trapped in discarded plastic or dying because they're unable to digest the plastic waste they've ingested. Even much of our bottled water contains microplastics. Humans are designed to contribute to the flourishing of the whole creation, but here we see the reverse. Tragically we sense little urgency to address the problem of plastic, and we have a hard time seeing how we can change before so much is destroyed.

Life is so beautiful but so broken. What went wrong?

Surprisingly, the most understandable answer comes through reflecting on our teenage years. For many of us they were a time of rebellion. Remember those years when you thought your parents were too involved in your life? Although still a teenager, you were brilliant—and your parents? Well, they were kind of clueless! You knew far better than they did what was best for you. Of course no parents are perfect and some are downright abusive, but this is very different from appropriate authority, which we all need. The Bible locates our deepest problem in just such rebellion against good authority.

To answer the question *What is wrong with our world?* we need to attend to the central relationship that's too easily ignored: our relationship with God. We are made above all else for relationship with God, but in our modern world we get distracted from this by so many things and activities and are so often determined to be the masters of our own destinies.

According to the Bible, this very desire to have absolute control over our lives, to be a law unto ourselves, is the root of the problem. God placed the first couple, Adam and Eve, in the perfect home, Eden. In Genesis 2 and 3, two trees right in the center of Eden are singled out as having huge symbolic value: the tree of life and the tree of the knowledge of good and evil (Genesis 2:9). Adam and Eve have all they need in the park, but they are forbidden to eat from the tree of the knowledge of good and evil.

Doubtless, you have never heard of a tree with such a name! Neither have we. This is because this tree is more than a tree; it is a symbol of a very different way of life than that intended by God for humans. God intends for humans to be gloriously and wonderfully alive; eating from this tree will bring *death* (Genesis 2:16-17). We find life when we submit to God and follow his ways in his world. This tree, however, stands for a decision that we know better than God; that we can choose for ourselves what is right and wrong; that, in fact, we can do a better job than God. In short, this tree stands for rebellion against God.

But how, you may ask, is this possible in a "very good" world? The answer is that part of the glory of being creatures made in the image of God is having free will. God, as we have seen, is personal, and he made us like him in this respect. He did not make us as robots who simply do what we are programmed to do. Rather, he gave us freedom to choose, and his deep desire is that we should choose to love him and to follow his will for our lives.

Enter the snake—Satan in disguise. He engages Eve in conversation, twisting God's words and getting her to see the forbidden tree as very attractive. He tells Eve that God lied; they will not die from eating the fruit of this tree. God is just jealous, says the serpent, for God knows that if they eat of it, they will become like God, and God doesn't want them to attain such power.

Eve looks, takes, eats. Then she gives some to her husband, Adam.

Much about the story of Adam and Eve's first sin is mysterious, but it is profound in its analysis of what happens to humans when they rebel against God, determined to live without him. In one sense, Satan is right. They do not immediately die, but part of what this story does is press us to think hard about what death really involves—not just physical death but relational breakdown.

We have seen that God created human beings to be in four basic relationships. The effect of the first couple's disobedience shatters all four relationships. Whereas before they were happily naked, now they feel shame and are self-conscious and quickly cover their nakedness, their shame. Whereas before they walked with God in Eden, now when they hear his approach, they quickly hide from him, just as we are prone to do when we have wronged someone we love. When God questions them, they refuse to take responsibility for their actions: Adam blames Eve and Eve blames the snake. Whereas in Genesis 1, God pronounced his blessing on them, now he pronounces his judgment on them and on the snake, and the first couple is banished from Eden with the way back barred by an angelic guard. Death includes physical death, but we learn here that life and death are about far more than physical life and death. None of these four relationships are completely destroyed, but all four are deeply damaged.

We can represent the effect of Adam and Eve's rebellion in Eden as seen in figure 4.1.

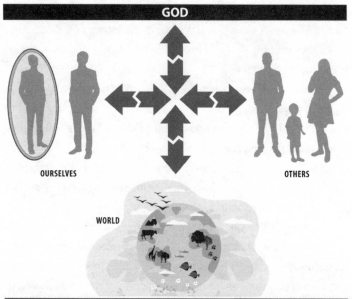

Figure 4.1. The four broken relationships

Once Adam and Eve are outside of Eden, they give birth to two boys, Cain and Abel. Abel grows up to be a shepherd and Cain a farmer. Human relationships with one another (marriage and family) and with the earth (shepherding and farming) continue, but soon we see the poison of rebellion against God in Cain, who becomes insanely jealous of Abel and ends up attacking him and killing him (Genesis 4:1-12). In a short time we have moved from the idyllic Eden to a horrific family murder. As the first couple and thus the great representatives of the human race, Adam and Eve have through their rebellion unleashed forces into the world that still swirl around and in us every day.

We have much to learn from the story of Adam and Eve's rebellion and its consequences. God is not like a great grandfather in the sky who, when we meet him after death, will simply ask, "Well, did you have a good time?" God is other than us and without sin, which he cannot tolerate. Sin means falling short of God's character and standards for humans. His love will not tolerate rebellion against and disobedience of his instructions, which have our best interests at heart.

But God does not abandon humans or his purposes with his creation. God continues to seek them out for conversation, to call them to good rather than broken and evil behavior, like that of Cain. And he continues to provide for them: Adam and Eve tried to cover themselves with leaves, but God provides proper, warm clothing for them from animal skins (Genesis 3:21). This is a sign that God in his extraordinary mercy has not given up on them, as we will see in the coming chapters.

We learn a lot about ourselves from this story too. The great twentieth-century Christian thinker and writer G. K. Chesterton got it right when he said, "What's wrong with the world? I am." Our very deepest problem is existing outside the relationship with God for which we are made.

READINGS: Genesis 3 and 4

5

OUT OF EDEN

Rebellion, Judgment, and Mercy

IF YOU REFER BACK to the introduction, you'll see that we provided you with a six-act outline of the drama of the Bible. In a relatively short space of time we have moved through acts one and two, "God Establishes His Kingdom: Creation" and "Rebellion in the Kingdom: Fall." As you will see from the header of this and following chapters, we now move into the long act three, "The King Chooses Israel: Salvation Initiated," which covers the rest of the Old Testament. How, you might be wondering, will God respond to the rebellion against him? In this chapter and the following ones we will find out.

So far we have seen that God is extraordinary. He is perfect and good and cannot tolerate rebellion against him; his very character rebels against it. And yet he is also merciful beyond measure, as we saw in the previous chapter in his provision of clothing for Adam and Eve.

Joe grew up with a father who was a rigid disciplinarian. Joe knew exactly what the rules were at home and the consequences—often severe—for breaking any of them. Joe experienced his father as distant, easily angered, and with no sense of Joe's fragile world. His father insisted, for example, that he have a military-style haircut unlike any of his fellow students at school. Joe was mocked endlessly for his extremely short hair—it was seriously out of fashion at the time—but there was nothing he could do about it.

Mary grew up, by comparison, with hippy parents in a household in which there were no rules. As a child she saw things she should never have seen and, lacking any boundaries, she developed into a selfish young person and later, an adult to whom rules of civility didn't apply. She was constantly pushing the margins in social and business settings, not understanding the consequences to her and others resulting from her behavior. In later life both Joe and Mary needed counseling to help them come to grips with the deficiencies in their childhoods and learn to develop healthy relationships.

These are fictional characters, but many of us know people just like Joe's father, who are strong disciplinarians but show little capacity for compassion and mercy. Or we know people like Mary's parents, who ooze with compassion but have little sense of the importance of boundaries and appropriate discipline.

Wonderfully God is not like us in this respect. In his character, justice and compassion are wonderfully balanced and work hand in hand. This is evident in Genesis 3–11, as events unfold once the first couple has been barred from Eden.

Adam and Eve's choice to defy God's warning despite all his goodness to them changed the course of history, as we have seen. But even amid his pronouncement of judgment on them and their descendents as well as on the snake (Satan), God makes an extraordinary promise to reverse what has gone wrong. When he pronounces judgment on the snake, God speaks these remarkable words:

> And I will put enmity
>> between you and the woman,
>> and between your offspring and hers;
> he will crush your head,
>> and you will strike his heel. (Genesis 3:15)

Adam and Eve sided with the snake when they ate from the forbidden fruit of the tree of the knowledge of good and evil, alienating themselves from God. Here, most remarkably, God promises that the day will come when he will reverse this situation by once again putting enmity between humans and the snake and thus restoring the original relationship between God and humans. A descendent of the first couple will crush the snake's head, and in the process the descendent's heel will be bitten.

This is a powerful image of God's deep commitment to his creation. Snakes are not evil; they are part of God's good creation. But as Craig knows well, having grown up in South Africa, certain snakes can be very dangerous, and that's the sort of snake representing Satan in this story. When we read these words, we should not have a harmless grass snake in mind but something more like the black mamba, one of the most feared snakes in Africa. Black mambas can grow up to fourteen feet long (between 2.5 and 4.5 meters). Their bite can be fatal, and they're incredibly

fast, capable of moving at more
than 12.5 miles (20 km) per hour.
Crushing the head of such a
snake with your heel, you'd be
very likely to pay the price of a
serious and life-threatening
bite—and that is the picture we
have here.

For good reason, Christians
see here the first promise of
Jesus, who we'll encounter later
in this story, as the one who will
come to deal decisively once
and for all with the effect of
human rebellion against God
(sin). As we will see when we get to that climactic point in the story of
the Bible, he will do this at great cost to himself. For now, the point is
that even as he is pronouncing judgment, God commits himself to the
recovery of his full and open relationship with humans.

God filled his creation with myriad hidden possibilities, and he intends for these to be developed by humans as they grow in numbers.
Despite human rebellion, we see in Genesis 4 the development of cities;
the origin of nomadic people; the development of musical instruments
and music; and the forging of tools from bronze and iron. It's hard for
us to imagine a world without music, in all its many forms a great gift
from God. Craig developed a new appreciation for the human development of metalworking, having taken several jewelry courses where

he learned to work with silver and gold and other metals. The rich potential built into God's creation takes time, skill, creativity, and effort to bring out. We also read in Genesis 4:26 that at this time people "began to call on the name of the LORD," a reference to the beginning of organized worship.

However, the effect of sin is that even as these developments take place they are continually twisted by sin. Poetry is a beautiful gift from God, but in Genesis 4:23-24, Lamech, a descendent of Cain, uses poetry as a vehicle to express the worst pride and the worst spirit of revenge:

I have killed a man for wounding me,
> a young man for injuring me.
If Cain is avenged seven times,
> then Lamech seventy-seven times.

We are familiar with the snowball effect: what starts as something small can soon become an avalanche. Evil and sin are like this, and in Genesis 1–11, despite God's grace, sin gathers momentum as it infects the minds and hearts of the developing human race. How will God respond?

God is wonderfully patient but not endlessly so. We know how dangerous the Ebola virus and more recently the coronavirus are; any outbreak has to be quarantined immediately. As sin spreads like a virus among humans, God decides to destroy most of the human race in a great flood and to start again, as it were, with one good man, Noah—"a righteous man, blameless among the people of his time, and he walked faithfully with God" (Genesis 6:9)—and his extended family. Noah's neighbors must have thought him quite mad. Under instruction from God, Noah builds a great big boat and takes into the boat his family and pairs of every type of animal and bird. When the flood comes, Noah, his family, and the animals are saved.

Some of us will be familiar with the story from our Sunday school days as a child. But it is far more than that. This story shows us just how seriously God takes sin, but it also displays his mercy and commitment to his creation. And God is not just concerned to save humankind but also the other creatures he made, the animals and the birds!

After the flood, God commissions Noah as a second Adam, commanding him—as he did Adam—to have a family and encourage his children to have families so that eventually the earth will be fully inhabited (Genesis 8:16-17). Intriguingly, however, whereas Adam and Eve were vegetarians, God now allows the animals to be eaten as food by Noah and his descendents. God establishes a legal agreement with Noah and his sons— what the Bible calls a "covenant"—never again to destroy the earth with such a flood and introduces the rainbow into the clouds as a sign of this covenant. The covenant is extended to include all living creatures.

We wait with bated breath to see what will happen now. Will Noah and his sons rise to the challenge and the opportunities presented to them? Alas, it is not long before the virus of sin is spreading again.

According to the Bible all nations of the earth descend from Noah's three sons: Shem, Ham, and Japheth. The growth of the human population and the development of nations with diverse languages is a good thing; it is part of what God intended for the development of his creation. But, as we know too well, nations have power, and sinful humans are only too prone to misuse power. And that is indeed what happens.

Just as Adam and Eve bought into Satan's lie that if they disobeyed God, they would become gods, so the nations conspire together as to how they can establish a twisted "United Nations" of their own and achieve great acclaim. At the heart of their enterprise they build a great tower, the Tower of Babel, designed to reach right up into God's abode in heaven. This is pride and arrogance on an international scale, again an attempt at being a law unto themselves and seeking equality with God. Full of irony, the Bible tells us that God still had to "come down" to see the tower! God's judgment is to scatter the nations across the earth and to make communication between nations difficult, so that they cannot ever conduct such an experiment again.

Genesis 4–11 is like two railway tracks running parallel to each other. On the one hand human rebellion gathers momentum until it threatens to overwhelm God's good creation. On the other hand the gracious and holy God punishes sin but remains committed to his creation. But this state of affairs seems unsustainable, and we are left wondering just what God will do to rectify the situation.

READINGS: Genesis 6 and 9

GOD'S SOLUTION

Abraham and His Descendents

A FEW YEARS AGO Craig spent just over a month in Jerusalem, staying at the Pontifical Biblical Institute just outside the walls of the old city. There he met a Roman Catholic priest with the most extraordinary story. From documentaries and films most of us have a sense of the chaos when America withdrew from Vietnam at the end of the Vietnam War, with so many desperately trying to get *out* of the country. This priest was sent on the last flight *into* Vietnam to be a priest there. He suffered imprisonment and persecution but survived. Craig had the privilege of hearing him preach from time to time in the lovely chapel at the Institute.

There are not many who would have accepted an assignment in such difficult circumstances, but as a faithful follower of God's calling, the priest obeyed not knowing what the future would hold.

This was a modern-day version of the call received by a much more elderly man many thousands of years before. This call came after God had disrupted humanity's latest efforts to become equal with God—the rebellious building of the Tower of Babel—scattering humankind across the earth and confusing their communication. God's positive response was to call an old man and his family to make a similarly incredible journey.

God called Abraham, already seventy-five, to uproot himself from his sophisticated, urban home in the city of Ur (today's southern Iraq) with his extended family, servants, and herds and to emigrate to a new land that God would lead him to, and where he would have to start life all over again.

Emigration of this sort is hard today. In Abraham's day, in which travel was slow and the extended family and the city were one's in-

surance, this was a radical and demanding call. One can only imagine what Abraham's friends and neighbors must have said to him: "Where exactly are you going?" "Do you know how dangerous such travel might be with all your herds and possessions?" "Here you are in this great city with such traditions and wealth. Why on earth would you leave it at your age?" Indeed, Abraham's journey was nothing less than a call to follow God into an unknown future. Doubtless those around Abraham must have wondered about his sanity.

God knows what a demanding call this is, and he gives Abraham three very significant promises. First, God promises that Abraham will have many, many descendents; indeed, God will make his descendents into *a great nation*. Late one night God takes Abraham outside, challenges him to count the stars, and promises him that his descendents would similarly be so numerous (Genesis 15:5). Second, God promises Abraham and his descendents that they will share a deep and special *relationship with God*. And third, God promises Abraham and his descendents *a land of their own*. These are wonderful promises, but they needed to be received with real faith and trust in God. Abraham's wife, Sarah, for example, was well beyond child-bearing age. How would they have even one descendent, let alone thousands? What would a special relationship with God look like, and how could God possibly give them a land of their own? Remarkably, Abraham trusted God and set out on this journey.

The call of Abraham and God's promises to him mark a major turning point in the biblical story. Up until now the focus of the story has been the nations of the world; here the focus narrows to the line of Abraham and his descendents. Having dispersed the nations of the world, we see God electing to form his own nation through Abraham. But why? Up until the call of Abraham in Genesis 12, the word *curse* or some form of it has been used five times to express God's anger as humans rebel against him (Genesis 3:14, 17; 4:11; 5:29; 9:25). The opposite of *curse* is *blessing*, representing God's original purpose for his creation to flourish and to be showered by his presence and gifts. In the compact three verses that tell of God's call of Abraham (Genesis 12:1-3), some form of the word *bless* occurs five times, deliberately set against the five occurrences of *curse* in Genesis 1–11.

What is the significance of this? The amazing point is that through what God is doing with Abraham, God will recover his purposes of blessing for all the nations of the world. Through Abraham, God says in Genesis 12:3, "all peoples on earth will be blessed."

Intriguingly we are given no details about how this will unfold. As with any good story, we'll have to wait to see how the plot develops, and doubtless there will be many surprises along the way. For now it's important to see that God's strategy of focusing his attention on one person is not an end in itself but will become the means for God's recovery of his purposes for the whole of his creation.

Why did God choose Abraham? We simply don't know. We watch with amazement as Abraham obeys God's call and sets out into the unknown. Perhaps, we might think, God chose him because he was particularly devout, a sort of ancient saint? Alas, as Abraham and his family's slow pilgrimage northwest and then south to the land of Canaan unfolds, we soon discover that Abraham is no saint but has serious faults like all of us.

Abraham and his household enter the land that God intends to give Abraham and his descendents, and they travel up and down it, symbolically laying claim to the whole even as they live outside the main cities in the margins. Yet time and again Abraham doubts God, who has to intervene to keep his plan on track. For example, when Abraham and his family are forced to go down to Egypt because of famine in Canaan, anxiety and panic get the better of Abraham.

Sarah is a very attractive woman, and Abraham fears that they will kill him in order to get hold of his wife. He thus has Sarah pretend to be his sister, with disastrous results. Pharaoh, the ruler of Egypt, adopts her into his harem, and God has to intervene to restore Sarah to Abraham (Genesis 12:10-20).

Abraham's faults are not the only obstacle. God has promised Abraham descendents like the myriad stars in the sky. There is only one problem: Abraham and his wife, Sarah, remain childless.

Again and again the story threatens to run into a dead end. Again and again God intervenes and renews his promises to Abraham. Against all odds and despite her lack of trust in God, Sarah becomes pregnant in her old age and gives birth to a son, Isaac. Isaac in turn marries, and the story focuses on one of his sons, Jacob, who himself has twelve sons, the ancestors of the twelve tribes that will make up the great nation God promised to Abraham.

The Bible devotes thirty-nine chapters (Genesis 12–50) to the lives of these three men and their families. Like Abraham, Isaac and Jacob also have serious faults, but God remains deeply engaged in their lives, forming them through their circumstances and their lack of trust so that they become mature people more worthy of and like the promise from God that they carry.

Probably the most searing story of this formation comes when Abraham is instructed to take Isaac and sacrifice him on Mount Moriah (Genesis 22). Has God gone completely mad? Isn't this a call to child sacrifice, the very worst practice of the nations in the Middle East of this time? It took so long for Sarah to conceive, and now God seems to be destroying everything. This time Abraham does not show his faults but instead reveals his extraordinary faith. Just as he left Ur and followed God's call, now he saddles up his donkey and heads off to Mount Moriah with his beloved son Isaac. What went through his head as he journeyed slowly those three long days toward the mountain? It is impossible to know. Just as he is about to slay Isaac, God tells Abraham to stop, and Abraham finds a ram—God's provision—to offer in Isaac's place.

This is a mysterious story. What are we to make of it? The storyteller provides us with an important clue: God was testing Abraham (Genesis 22:1). It is part of God's formation of Abraham. To be formed to become like the promise he had been given, Abraham needs to be willing to relinquish the promise itself. Without Isaac he would have no descendents!

God's involvement with Abraham tells us a lot about God. Doubtless, like Abraham, we may have our own idea of how things should work when we encounter God. When God gets involved in our lives, we have an idea of his developing the house of our life into a delightful beach cottage! And then God starts breaking walls down! God has something much more expansive in mind as part of his purposes for the world. He is a surprising God, certainly a loving God—but nevertheless he is God, and we are not.

This chapter is titled "God's Solution: Abraham and His Descendents." Abraham and his descendents are the solution but only by God's grace and mercy. This will become apparent as we turn to Isaac's son Jacob and his twelve sons.

READINGS: Genesis 12; 18:1-15; 22

JACOB, JOSEPH,
AND HIS BROTHERS

NOWADAYS IN WESTERN SOCIETY we are used to
things moving very fast. People fly around the world and
get frustrated if their phones and tablets are offline for a few hours.
God, by comparison, works out his purposes slowly and steadily. He
promised Abraham many descendents who would have a land of
their own and a special relationship with God himself, but it would
take hundreds of years for these promises to be fulfilled. In the
process God remains graciously and deeply involved with Abraham
and his line.

George Stephanopoulos wrote a book about President Bill
Clinton called *All Too Human*. And so it is with Abraham, his son
Isaac, and his grandson Jacob. At times they show remarkable trust
in God, but too often they follow their own desires and plans and

end up in dangerous situations. The good news is that God remains deeply at work amid their folly, steadily achieving his purposes through them.

Jacob and Esau were twin brothers, both sons of Isaac (grandsons of Abraham). Esau was the older one and thus the main heir. In those days the oldest son received the blessing from his father as the heir apparent. Jacob, however, desperately wanted this blessing for himself. He deceived his father, Isaac, who was old and blind, into thinking that he, Jacob, was Esau, thereby deceitfully receiving the blessing. Not surprisingly Esau was very angry about this, and Jacob and Esau became alienated from each other. To avoid the fate of Abel (who, as you may recall from chapter four, was killed by his brother Cain out of jealousy), Jacob fled far away and lived in fear of Esau's revenge (Genesis 27:41-45).

Astonishingly, God gets involved and works out his purposes in the lives of such broken people as Jacob. Amid Jacob's immaturity and stupidity, God meets with him at crucial moments in his life.

A wonderful example is what happened to Jacob one night after he had fled from Esau. Spending the night out in the open, he found a stone for a pillow and slept. In a remarkable dream he saw a ladder extending from the earth right into heaven, with angels ascending and descending on it. At the top of the ladder stood God, and God repeated his promises to Jacob that had been originally given to Abraham—namely, possessing the land, producing many descendents, enjoying a special relationship with God, and becoming a blessing to the nations (Genesis 28:10-22). When he woke up, Jacob was amazed and declared that this place was the house of God, the gate of heaven. He gave it the Hebrew name "Bethel," which means "the house of God."

On another occasion, just before Jacob was to encounter Esau again for the first time since leaving, he was alone, stressed and afraid, and had a strange experience of wrestling with a man right through the night (Genesis 32:22-32). As they wrestled, Jacob's hip was damaged. Only at the end of this long night did Jacob realize he had been wrestling with God, who blessed him, thus preparing him for his meeting with Esau.

Jacob called this place "Peniel," meaning "the face of God" because he saw God and survived! If he could survive such a night, then he could survive meeting up with his brother again. God also changed Jacob's name to "Israel," which probably means "he struggles with God." Israel will become the name, too, of the people of God who would descend from Jacob.

Despite having such profound experiences of God, Jacob was not the wisest father. He had twelve sons, but Joseph was his favorite. He made an ornate robe for Joseph, a constant visual reminder of Jacob's favoritism and a thorn in the flesh for Joseph's brothers. One day Joseph had a dream of all his brothers bowing down to him. Foolishly he told his brothers about his dream, which enraged them and increased their jealousy. Like Cain with Abel, this jealousy smoldered into a fire, and, when the opportunity arose, they made plans to kill Joseph. Seizing him, they threw him into a water hole, leaving him there to die. Shortly afterward, however, they saw merchants passing by and realized it would be far better to sell him as a slave to the merchants. They could not have known the merchants would later sell him in Egypt to Potiphar, an official of the king (Pharaoh) of Egypt.

The young, spoiled Joseph must have wondered what on earth would happen to him. Little did he know he was in for a roller coaster of a ride. Initially he prospered under Potiphar. But when he refused to have sex with Potiphar's wife, who was attracted to Joseph by his good looks, she falsely accused him of attempted rape. He was thrown into prison, where over the course of several years he gained a reputation for being able to interpret dreams. When he alone, with God's help, was able to interpret a dream of Pharaoh's about seven years of prosperity followed by seven years of severe famine, Pharaoh took him out of prison and into royal service. Now only thirty years old, Joseph was made second in command over Egypt, tasked to prepare for the coming famine.

Joseph had many dark moments in his life. He must often have felt abandoned by his family and by God; why must he suffer so very

much? However, he later came to see—and his story is a wonderful example of this—that God was at work in all his immaturity as well as the stupidity and jealousy of Jacob and his brothers, just as he is in our own lives. Joseph established great silos to store food during the seven years of prosperity so that when the famine struck, and it was very severe, there was sufficient food to feed the Egyptians.

The famine struck far beyond Egypt and extended into Canaan, where Jacob and his sons and their families lived. Ironically, in desperation Jacob sent his sons to ask for food from Egypt. On their second such journey, they meet with Joseph himself, who upon seeing them broke down in tears. Like Jacob when he had been about to meet Esau, Joseph's brothers were terrified, but the now mature Joseph spoke the most extraordinary words:

> Do not be distressed and do not be angry with yourselves for selling me here, because it was to save lives that God sent me ahead of you. . . . So then, it was not you who sent me here, but God. He made me father to Pharaoh, lord of his entire household and ruler of all Egypt. (Genesis 45:5-8)

There are so many harrowing elements in Joseph's story: unwise parental favoritism with catastrophic consequences, jealousy that led to murderous intent, being sold into slavery, falling foul of the petty rage of Potiphar's wife, years in prison, and so on. Such suffering must at many points have led to Joseph asking why, just as we do when things go wrong in our lives. But Joseph came to see that God was at work amid all the injustice and chaos of his life, even when God seemed completely absent. God's control of history, steadily pursuing his purposes even when we cannot see them, never detracts from our responsibility for our bad behavior. But it is truly wonderful to know that God is on the throne and that—amid all we go through—he works for our good and for the fulfillment of his purposes.

Because of Joseph's favored position in Egypt, not only did Jacob and his sons and their families not starve, but they were also granted permission to settle in Egypt, where they prospered and grew. Indeed, they and their descendents stayed in Egypt for some four hundred years, during which time their numbers multiplied rapidly. By the end of this time God's promise to Abraham that he would have many descendents was fulfilled. But the Israelites were in Egypt, not in Canaan, their Promised Land. How would the other two promises to Abraham be fulfilled? The next chapter tells that part of the story.

READINGS: Genesis 28:10-22 and 45:1-28

OUT OF EGYPT

I N THE UNITED KINGDOM, four hundred years does not seem like such a long time since the history of the United Kingdom goes back so far. Craig lives in the Fens north of Cambridge, a relatively young part of the United Kingdom since it was only drained in the seventeenth century! In most of America, four hundred years seems like a long time, since the United States is a relatively young country. Either way, you tend to get settled after four hundred years in a place (see Genesis 15:13-16), and it was like that for the Israelites. Being under the protection of Pharaoh and flourishing and growing as they were, many must have thought, *Why not just stay here in Egypt where we are? Life is good here!* But, of course, this was not God's plan for his people. His intention as told to Abraham was for them to live in their own land under one king, himself. But had the Israelites remembered God's promise to Abraham, or had their memories dimmed as the years passed?

Early on in the second book of the Bible, Exodus, we read these ominous words: "Then a new king, to whom Joseph meant nothing, came to power in Egypt" (Exodus 1:8). In Egypt the Pharaoh was regarded as a god, and his power was absolute. Like the many gods in whom the Egyptians believed, Pharaoh was capable of feeling threatened and of acting capriciously and ruthlessly. As he surveyed the growth of the Israelites, this is exactly how he felt. His solution was twofold: first, make life as unpleasant as possible for them by enslaving them, and second, institute a policy of infanticide. He instructed the Hebrew midwives to attend closely to every child born to the Israelites and, if the child was a boy, to kill the baby. Amazingly, the midwives feared God above Pharaoh and disobeyed Pharaoh's dreadful instructions. Pharaoh's response reveals his depravity: he instructed the Egyptians to hurl every Hebrew boy into the Nile River, an unimaginable horror.

This is brutal oppression of the worst sort, and we might well wonder, *What hope is there for the Israelites?* Their hope is, of course, in God, but is he up to the challenge of the political and military might and power of Pharaoh? The stage is set for a showdown between the god-Pharaoh and the God of the Israelites. And what a showdown it is.

To try to save her baby son, a young Israelite mother puts her boy, Moses, in a waterproof basket and hides him amid the reeds along the banks of the Nile (Exodus 2:1-10). Astonishingly, one of Pharaoh's own daughters discovers him and has compassion on him. She rescues Moses and has him nurtured by his mother until he can live in Pharaoh's court and receive the best education in the land! Moses, when he is grown up, is the one God will call to liberate his people from the oppression of Egypt. Ironically, he is trained and educated to be a leader in Pharaoh's own palace, right under Pharaoh's nose!

However, despite living the good life in Pharaoh's palace, Moses never forgets that he is an Israelite. One day, after becoming an adult, Moses goes out to where the enslaved Israelites are working, and he sees an Egyptian beating up an Israelite. Enraged, Moses intervenes and kills the Egyptian. The news reaches Pharaoh's ears, and too late he tries to have Moses killed. Moses flees for his life to Midian, where he finds a home with a priest called Reuel and his seven daughters. Moses marries one of the daughters and settles into life as a shepherd (Exodus 2:11-22).

Years later Moses is, as usual, leading his flocks to pasture, this time around a mountain called Sinai, when something extraordinary happens (Exodus 3). He notices that a bush is burning, and yet strangely it is not incinerated. He goes closer to take a look at this unusual occurrence, just as any one of us would surely do, and God himself calls to Moses from the bush. Moses answers, "Here I am." God instructs Moses not to come any closer and to take off his shoes because the ground he stands on is holy. In total contrast to ruthless Pharaoh, God tells Moses,

> I have indeed seen the misery of my people in Egypt. I have heard them crying out because of their slave drivers, and I am concerned about their suffering. So I have come down to rescue them from the hand of the Egyptians and to bring them up out of that land into a good and spacious land. . . . So now, go. I am sending you to Pharaoh to bring my people the Israelites out of Egypt. (Exodus 3:7-10)

Moses finds every excuse he can muster to avoid this commission. God assures him that he himself will be with Moses. He also reveals his own name to be Yahweh (normally translated as "LORD" in our Bible) to Moses. The name means "I will be what I will be," a profound assurance that God will act for the Israelites in a way that is consistent with his compassionate character (Exodus 3; compare Exodus 6:1-9). Moses' last excuse is that he is not a good public speaker. God tells him to take his bother Aaron along to do the speaking.

By this time the Pharaoh who sought to have Moses killed has died, but his replacement is no better. What follows is a repeated confrontation between Moses and the new Pharaoh, but Pharaoh refuses to yield. Pharaoh's response to their first meeting is to ramp up the oppression of the Israelites. An escalating clash between Moses and Pharaoh ensues.

One by one God unfurls nine plagues upon Egypt. The first two relate specifically to the Nile River: the Nile turns to blood, and then the Nile, and thus all of Egypt, becomes infested with frogs. The Nile was the lifeblood of Egypt, and as a god, Pharaoh was responsible for its well-being. Plagues of gnats and flies; a disease affecting all livestock; plagues of boils, hail, and locusts; and darkness follow. None of these plagues would have been totally unfamiliar to the Egyptians, but their immensity and timing are miraculous.

Through Moses, God tells Pharaoh, "I have raised you up for this very purpose, that I might show you my power and that my name might be proclaimed in all the earth" (Genesis 9:16). Astonishingly, God in his boundless generosity appears to offer Pharaoh and thus Egypt the possibility of becoming part of his people. In Exodus 4:22 when Moses is instructed to tell Pharaoh, "Israel is my firstborn son. . . . Let my son go," God may be implying to Pharaoh that he is open to having other sons as well, sons such as Egypt. But Pharaoh will have none of it, and as God says in Exodus 4:23, the final devastating plague will therefore be the death of every firstborn son and animal in Egypt.

The terrible deaths of the final plague will at the same time mark the birth of the people Israel. Moses instructs the Israelites that this month will be the first month in their new calendar once they leave Egypt. Each household is to slaughter a lamb and to paint blood on their front doors, so that the angel of death will *pass over* their houses when the final and most terrible plague falls. The feast to commemorate God's deliverance will henceforth be called the Passover.

The final plague breaks Pharaoh, and he lets the Israelites go. Moses leads them out of Egypt toward the Red Sea. Pharaoh then changes his mind and sends his armies after the departing nation, now caught between the Red Sea and Pharaoh's approaching armies. One can only imagine the panic and terror of the malnourished and exhausted Israelites. But Yahweh is with them, and at God's command, Moses raises his staff and the sea divides so that the Israelites can escape through it. The Egyptians follow them into the sea but are engulfed as the waters return (Exodus 14).

Free at last! The people of Israel still have a long journey ahead of them, but they are free from the tyranny of Pharaoh and the Egyptians. Songs of celebration are composed, and the Israelites sing,

> I will sing to the LORD,
>> for he is highly exalted.
> Both horse and driver
>> he has hurled into the sea. . . .
> The LORD reigns
>> for ever and ever. (Exodus 15:1, 18)

Against all the odds of Pharaoh's military might and power, the Israelites experience an extraordinary escape, a rescue by God. The word for this rescue is *exodus*, hence the name of the second book of the Bible, Exodus. They are free *from* Egypt, but what will happen next to this group of former slaves? Read on.

READINGS: Exodus 3 and 15:1-21

MEETING WITH GOD

ISRAEL'S JOURNEY THROUGH the wilderness is long and hard, but God's intention is to establish them as his people and then lead them into a land where, under his guidance, they can set up a healthy society with hundreds of good neighborhoods—neighborhoods where there is no kidnapping, no murder, no stealing, no lying, and no giving false testimony under oath. This is good news!

Israel's deliverance from slavery in Egypt was truly miraculous, an act of God on behalf of an oppressed nation. In Exodus 19 God says their deliverance is like an eagle flying with its young on its back. God, we might say today, has an airline, Air Yahweh, and it piloted the Israelites to safety out of Egypt. But what was its destination? God's answer in Exodus 19:4 is "and [I] brought you to myself"—a profound expression of relationship!

Of course, once the Israelites left Egypt they were in the wilderness, and we all know that traveling in the wilderness by foot is no fun. It's not the sort of holiday we go looking for on the internet! It's very hot during the day and often icy cold at night; you never know what snakes and other wild animals you might encounter. And what are we going to eat and drink? God provided food for the Israelites each day. In the morning, there was a flaky type of bread called *manna* on the ground, and in the evening, he sent quails for meat.

When we get to Jesus in the New Testament, we will see that he taught his disciples a prayer that you might already know, the Our Father or Lord's Prayer. One request in this short prayer is "Give us this day our daily bread," a reminder to everyone who prays it that we are dependent each day on God for what we need that day.

God was teaching the same lesson to the Israelites. Even though the Israelites had just experienced the most remarkable deliverance from terrible oppression, they were not averse to grumbling. Moses led them and God was clearly with them, but life in the wilderness was no holiday resort. God provided for their basic needs, but some wondered when the banquets of delicious food would arrive and started to look back to Egypt with some misgivings about where they were headed.

Where were they headed? They journeyed to the same region where Moses first encountered Yahweh in the burning bush. A mountain called Sinai is there, and the Israelites, at Moses' command, camped around the mountain. Moses told the Israelites to get ready. In three days they were going to meet God! Of course it was not as though the people were unfamiliar with God. After all, he had rescued them from Egypt, and he had accompanied them and led them on their journey to Mount Sinai in a pillar of cloud by day and a pillar of fire by night. But remember, it was Moses who had personal dealings with Yahweh, and now the whole people needed to be formally introduced to Yahweh so that they could get a sense of who he is, what his plans were for them, and what they would need to do to be part of those plans.

God had brought the Israelites to himself; he wanted to be their God and to live in their midst as their King, recovering the relationship he had with Adam and Eve in Eden. But if this wonderful possibility was to be achieved, then they needed to know clearly what he is like and what his conditions were for living among them.

We can only imagine the conversations among the Israelites during those three days of waiting to meet God. From their time in Egypt they were familiar with religion, but their recent experience told them that Yahweh was very different from the many Egyptian gods. Had he not overcome Pharaoh, who was himself a god? Most Egyptian gods exercised only local authority, but Yahweh had traveled with them on their journey; clearly Yahweh could not be confined to a temple or to one town or country. They could tell that God was with them, but why did they not have an image of him like the Egyptian gods? Whatever their thoughts and conversations, nothing prepared them for God's arrival.

C. S. Lewis evokes the reality of God by comparison to a game of burglars played by children. All is fun and well until we hear a footstep that we can't identify. Game over! The last thing we want is a real burglar, and many of us are like that with religion. A big, grandfather figure in the sky who will say to us at the pearly gates, "Well, did you have a good time?" we can live with. But the living God—why, that is another story.

And so it was with the Israelites. On the third day Mount Sinai was covered in smoke and fire and lightning as God descended upon it. Moses had encountered God in the burning bush; now the whole mountain was ablaze. Moses had set up boundaries around the mountain that were not to be crossed, but at least initially he need not have worried. The people were terrified. Instinctively the Israelites realized they were in the presence of the uncreated God. Instinctively they were aware of his holiness and their own sinfulness. To come into God's presence can be frightening, and doubtless the Israelites feared that God would destroy them. Indeed, when God spoke to them from the mountain, they were so terrified that they asked Moses to mediate between them and God and to tell them what God was saying rather than have God speak to them directly.

God *is* scary. The word in the Bible for that is *holy*. He is the uncreated God, the origin of all things, without sin and perfectly good. He is also extraordinarily gracious, as we have seen in his listening to the desperate cries of the oppressed. And when Yahweh does speak and explain to the Israelites what he has in mind for them, his plan could not have been better. God intended that the Israelites would become his people, live under his rule with him in their midst, and develop communal and individual lives that reflect his character. In this way they would show to the world what life really looks like when it is lived according to the designer's plan. What could be more wonderful?

We often hear people today lauding unconditional love as though all of us are angels just waiting for our goodness to break forth. Unconditional love sounds fine until you encounter people who murder or rape others, people who lie through their teeth in courts of law, people who are greedy and want everything we have. In the face of such behavior, unconditional love soon wises up to the fact that real love has boundaries. And this is what God in his great love explains to the Israelites at Mount Sinai. God is ready to forgive if his people turn back to him, but his patience has limits. If they want to be his people and to be part of his extraordinary plan for his world, then they will need to sign up to follow his rules. At the heart of his rules that he sets out at Sinai are the Ten Commandments (Exodus 20; Deuteronomy 5), which are a pithy summary of what is required of the Israelites if they are going to be part of God's people.

The Ten Commandments naturally divide into two parts: our relationship with God and our relationship with our neighbors. Because of who he is, God is by nature and rightly jealous, in the sense that he will not tolerate the Israelites worshiping other gods. They are to worship him alone. And just as God is gracious and merciful, so, too, they are made in his image to reflect his character. They are to love their neighbors, resisting and avoiding destructive practices like committing adultery or murder, giving false testimony in courts of law, and seeking to have what belongs to their neighbors.

The Ten Commandments often get bad press as though they are a kind of killjoy, sucking all the fun and joy out of life. In fact they are the opposite. As one writer says of them, they describe the ethos of the good neighborhood! Imagine a neighborhood in which there was no murder, a neighborhood in which you could trust police and courts of law to always act for justice, a neighborhood where you need have no fear that anyone would steal your property. A neighborhood like the one we described at the beginning of this chapter. Such a neighborhood would be a delight, one in which children could wander safely, one in which doors of houses could be left unlocked without fear of burglary, one in which family life flourished, one in which we would have no fear of yet another gun attack at a local school. This helps us to understand why God's love has boundaries. His ways are ways for human flourishing, and if we continually reject them, the danger is that eventually God will let us have our own way and allow us to pursue ways of death rather than of life.

At Sinai God's people agree to God's terms, and they are established in a formal, legal relationship with him, which the Bible calls a *covenant*. In it, this all-powerful God declares his love and care for them, and in return the people accept his requirement to love him and love one another, showing it by their actions. Not surprisingly, the Bible likens this covenant relationship to a marriage and the similarities are instructive. Of course, a marriage is about far more than the law, but marriage is so important and so binding that cementing it in a legal way is important and helpful. So it is with the

Israelites. What God is offering them is amazing, but it is also very serious, and they need to reflect hard on what they are agreeing to. This God of fire and lightning and thunder is going to be living in their midst as their King. They do agree to God's conditions and the stage is set for God to move in their midst. But we know how prone the Israelites are to falter and stop trusting God. If God's love is not unconditional, what will happen if they rebel against him? Our story continues.

READINGS: Exodus 19 and 20

GOD MOVES IN NEXT DOOR

THE PEOPLE OF THE United Kingdom take royalty very seriously. Imagine a royal marriage with huge crowds—some of whom have camped out all night—gathered along the streets to catch a glimpse of the royal couple. Millions more sit with their eyes glued to the TV or buy the magazines that cover the event. Part of the attraction is that such events are like fairy tales: fabulous costumes, beautiful carriages, sumptuous celebrations—far removed from the humdrum of our day-to-day lives. Very few of us have access to such a world, and it is simply unimaginable that such a royal couple would move into our ordinary neighborhood. No, they live in wonderful, secure houses on vast estates as part of the cultural elite.

It would be a huge shock if a royal couple—say the Queen and Prince Philip—moved in next door. And yet, this is just the sort of thing that happened to the Israelites. It would be hard to imagine a more unlikely group for this to happen to. The Israelites were—until very recently—oppressed and enslaved, the dirt of Egyptian society. They had almost nothing to recommend themselves. In his mercy, the LORD had heard their cries and rescued them from their slavery, and through Moses' and Aaron's leadership, God brought them to Mount Sinai where he descended on the mountain, spoke face-to-face with Moses for some forty days, and formed them legally into his people. Having made sure that they understood what being his people would entail—namely, living under *his* rule according to *his* rules, God formally established them in a covenant relationship with himself, much like a marriage is formalized in a public ceremony.

After the formation of the covenant, the leaders of Israel ascend Mount Sinai and enjoy a meal in the presence of God:

> Moses and Aaron, Nadab and Abihu, and the seventy elders of Israel went up and saw the God of Israel. Under his feet was something like a pavement made of lapis lazuli, as bright blue as the sky. But God did not raise his hand against these leaders of the Israelites; they saw God, and they ate and drank. (Exodus 24:9-11)

A meal with the King of kings! How extraordinarily gracious! But far more follows. Moses remains on the mountain for forty days, during which time God gives him precise instructions about the portable house the Israelites are to build for God (Exodus 24–31). You can always tell a really important part in a story because the storyteller slows the narrative down, and this is exactly what happens in the Bible at this point. There are many chapters with God's instructions for building his portable house and then many chapters explaining how these instructions were carried out. Although as readers we might find the repetition tedious, the story slows because what is going on is so momentous. The King of kings and the Lord of lords is having a house built to live in amid his people, meaning he will accompany them on their journey to the land he has promised them!

As we would expect, the furniture in God's portable house, called the *tabernacle*, is in some ways much like that of any house: there is a chair (called the mercy seat), a table, and a lampstand. Of course, in other ways it is unlike any normal house. The details of each otherwise-ordinary item are designed to remind the people that the King of kings lives there. The box beneath the mercy seat contains the stone tablets of the covenant on which God himself had written the Ten Commandments before giving them to Moses on the mountain. The box (called the Ark of the Covenant) is overlaid with gold inside and out; even the rings attached to the box so that it can be carried are made of gold, as is the elaborate lampstand. The perimeter of the tabernacle is fashioned of brightly colored curtains: blue, purple, and red, with angels woven into them. Gold is for royalty and angels for heaven; with the tabernacle heaven has come down to earth; God will live among human beings! In some ways God's portable house is similar to the temples the Israelites encountered in Egypt. In one huge way it is radically different: there is no statue of God in the tabernacle! God is the living God—he cannot be contained in a statue or represented by one.

In the UK if you visit one of the Queen's residences, you will soon discover that parts of the castle are out of bounds and carefully guarded. It was the same with God's house. As you can see from figure 10.1 of the tabernacle, the place where God sits was called the holy of holies—that is, the most holy place. God says of this place: "There . . . I will meet with you [Moses] and give you all my commands" (Exodus 25:22). There are gradations of specialness in God's tabernacle, from the holy of holies to the holy place to the Outer Court.

The two altars and the table and the bronze basin, or laver, alert us to the fact that God's tabernacle is far more than an ordinary house. He is the great King and this place will be the focal point of his people's worship of him.

God's plan to live amid his people is a sign of his extraordinary willingness to come down to their level, demonstrating his great love for them. Imagine waking up each morning and looking out of your tent to see . . . God's house

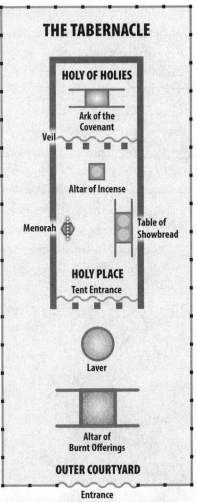

Figure 10.1. Diagram of God's house, the tabernacle

in your midst! At the same time God's presence is dangerous because of the Israelites' immaturity and tendency to rebel against God.

Indeed, even while Moses is up the mountain with God for forty days receiving the instructions about God's house, the Israelites become anxious waiting for Moses to return and lapse into the most awful idolatry. Aaron forges a calf out of gold for them, and they worship it. God threatens his people—they have broken the first commandment: "You shall have no other gods besides me!"—and Moses has to intercede with God not to destroy them. Here we witness in the Israelites our all too human tendency to worship things other than the living God. God relents and the covenant is renewed, but it is a close shave and raises concerns about the future.

Wisely God instructs Moses to appoint priests who will take re-sponsibility for the daily operation of the tabernacle and who will

function as a kind of diplomatic corps, mediating between God and the people. In Leviticus—the third book of the Bible—we find God's in-structions for the priests, given so they will know exactly what to do when things go wrong as well as how to function in the tabernacle. Seeing how easily the Israelites fell into idolatry, clearly the priests are in-tended to play a crucial role in keeping the relationship between God and his people healthy.

Finally the tabernacle is completed and assembled. Then a great cloud covers the tabernacle, and God's glory—his presence—fills it so that not even Moses is able to enter it. God takes up residence among his people.

Of course, the people know God's presence is so great that he cannot possibly be contained by a tabernacle. And yet we must not think that the tabernacle was just a symbol of God's presence amidst his people. God is truly present among them as their King. Indeed, only when the cloud over the tabernacle lifts do they journey on; if it does not lift, they stay put. At night the cloud is like fire. The cloud and the fire remind the people of Mount Sinai—the God the Israelites encountered there now has a house and is living in their midst.

READING: Exodus 40

THE LAND

I F YOU ARE LIKE the two of us, who travel a fair bit, then you may find traveling by air nowadays boring and tedious. With all the added security, air travel includes not only long flights with limited leg room but hours at the airport before flying, possible flight delays, jetlag, and so on.

When Craig lived in Canada and was returning to South Africa for a holiday, he would regularly fly through the night from Toronto to London Heathrow, wait all day at the airport, then take another long flight through the night to Johannesburg, and then a short flight from Johannesburg to Durban. The overnight flight to Heathrow was the killer. Losing five or six hours is no fun, and then spending the whole day at the airport waiting for the evening flight to Johannesburg felt like adding insult to injury. As much as he was looking forward to being back in South Africa, it was hard not to be grumpy en route. Tiredness brings out the worst in us.

And so it was with the Israelites. They were now on the way to the land that God promised to give them, and God was visibly present in their midst. Before they left Sinai to begin their journey to the Promised Land, God had Moses take a census of the male Israelites. The reason for the census was so that they would know how many men were available to fight alongside God in taking possession of the land promised to them. The men would need to function as an army once they reached the land. Of course they had not been trained to be soldiers, and it's hard to imagine anything less like a disciplined army than the Israelites. God was leading them on their way, but traveling by foot through wilderness desert, day after day, is no fun, and it wasn't long before the complaints began again.

When things go wrong in our lives, it is astonishing how quickly we romanticize the past! Israel had a terrible time in Egypt: they were enslaved, mistreated, starved, oppressed. Now they were free and God was with them, but still the grumbling began—or should we say continued? Ever since the Israelites left Egypt, God had provided food and water for them. This was a nutritious diet but predictable and even boring. And so the grumbling began: "If only we had proper meat to eat! Remember the delicious fish roasted over the fire in Egypt. Oh! Yes! And the cucumbers, melons, leeks, onions, and garlic" (see Numbers 11:5). Amid the hardship of the wilderness you would find Israelites in tears, wishing they were back in Egypt where the daily menu was so much better! Why on earth did they follow Moses out of Egypt only to land in this horrible place? Dissatisfaction with the menu leads to dissatisfaction with the leadership, and a group arises challenging Moses' leadership of the Israelites. Now, of course, this was seriously dangerous territory for the Israelites. God lived in their midst, and they had agreed to be his people according to his rules. When God heard their grumbling, Moses had to intercede for them lest God punish them for their lack of trust in God and his appointed leader, Moses.

For their journey ahead and the wonderful mission to which God has called them, the Israelites need to be a people with deep trust in God. When they come to the borders of the Promised Land, Moses, following God's instruction, sends spies into the land to scout it out. After forty days the spies return, reporting that the land flowed with milk and honey and bringing samples of the delicious fruit to show the Israelites. They could taste how good the land was! But the report is mixed (see Numbers 13:30-33): the inhabitants of the land were strong, and some were so big that the spies felt like grasshoppers next to them!

Once again the Israelites fail the test of trust. If a pessimist sees a glass as half empty and an optimist as half full, the Israelites are thoroughly pessimistic. They see the glass as nearly empty and behave like spoiled children, weeping and complaining and even wishing they had died in Egypt rather than be defeated by the inhabitants of the land ahead of them. Again Moses intercedes for them and they are forgiven, but there are consequences for their lack of trust. God declares that none of the current generation will enter the land. For forty years—approximately the length of a generation—the Israelites are to wander in the wilderness as the generation that left Egypt dies out.

After forty long years God leads the new generation of Israelites once again to the borders of the Promised Land. Moses knows (because God has told him) that he himself will die before they enter the land. His last task is to prepare the Israelites for life in the land that God is about to give them. The book of Deuteronomy—literally the "second law"—contains a record of Moses' sermons to the Israelites. It reviews the journey they had been on, reminding them of God's goodness to them, reiterating the rules of their (covenant) relationship with God, and urging them to trust God and obey his laws, to learn from their past mistakes and not to repeat them.

As the time draws near for the people to enter Canaan, God commissions Joshua, one of the spies who had reconnoitered the land forty years before, as their new leader. Shortly thereafter, the Lord speaks to Moses telling him to go up to Mount Nebo where he can see the Promised Land. There he will die and be gathered to his people. Joshua will lead the Israelites as they conquer the inhabitants of the land God has promised to the Israelites. Canaan is a small land of only about eight thousand square miles (twenty thousand square kilometers) including the inhabitable area to the east of the River Jordan, about the size of El Salvador, Slovenia, or New Jersey today. On the west it is bordered by the Mediterranean Sea and on the east and south, by desert. Valleys and mountain ranges carve up the land into many different parcels. Canaan is sandwiched between the great empires of Egypt and Mesopotamia with trade routes running through it.

Canaan is not, of course, uninhabited, and to possess the land, Joshua has to lead the Israelites in conquering the territory and defeating its inhabitants, which he does. The dispossession of the land from its former inhabitants, described in the book of Joshua, is especially controversial today. It remains a mystery, but the Bible gives us some important clues. At the outset of the conquest Joshua has a telling experience (Joshua 5:13-15). Joshua is near the ancient city of Jericho and he sees a man standing with his sword drawn. As a good military commander Joshua interrogates him: "Are you with us or our enemies?" The man's answer is revealing: "Neither, . . . but as commander of the army of the LORD I have now come." Only with God's help are the Israelites to conquer the land, and the Bible stresses that God had been patient with the inhabitants of the land despite their many evil practices, but his patience had run out (see Genesis 15:16).[1]

By the end of the book of Joshua, after multiple battles that you can read about there, Israel is established in the land with each of the twelve tribes assigned their own territory. Back in chapter six we mentioned that God had promised to give Abraham many descendents, to be in relationship with them, and to give them a land of their own. All these promises are now fulfilled. Israel is in her own land with God living in her midst! It is a dream come true. The potential and opportunities are tremendous. Will Israel now live up to them? Given her past, the prospects are not promising.

READINGS: Joshua 1 and 24:1-28

12

NO KING IN ISRAEL

I (CRAIG) GREW UP IN SOUTH AFRICA in a very sporty family. But until I came to America, I had never encountered a sport like American football, let alone the Super Bowl and all the wonderful craziness that is associated with it. In Africa we all know a football is round and you kick it! We also call it soccer. Now imagine that you're an American football fanatic and you've moved to Africa at the exact same time American football was introduced there. Not only would you likely be a star player, but you would have inside knowledge of the game that none of the locals possess: a recipe, we would say, for success.

The Israelites were now in a similar position. Of course, the land was new to them, but their God is the Creator of heaven and earth, and no one knows better how life works than God. God is only too keen to share his wisdom with his people. As Moses told them,

> See, I have taught you decrees and laws as the LORD my God commanded me, so that you may follow them in the land you are entering to take possession of it. Observe them carefully, for this will show your wisdom and understanding to the nations, who will hear about all these decrees and say, "Surely this great nation is a wise and understanding people." What other nation is so great as to have their gods near them the way the LORD our God is near us whenever we pray to him? (Deuteronomy 4:5-7)

With God on their side, Israel's new start in the land should have been a recipe for success!

Israel is now indeed settled in the land of milk and honey. No more manna and quail (see Joshua 5:12)! An immense opportunity now lies before them. Despite all their lack of trust and repeated failures, God has been wonderfully faithful to the once-enslaved people he rescued from Egypt. How will the Israelites respond now that they are in their own land? Each tribe has its own area assigned under Joshua. Together they make up the one people of God called to live in the land under his reign and to be a showcase to the other nations of what human life looks like in all its dimensions—political, economic, agricultural, familial, religious, and the like—when it is lived as God intended it to be. This is the first time in history that a nation came into existence with this mission to the world!

However, moving into a new country is not easy. I have lived in South Africa (where I grew up), in Canada, in the UK, and in America. Moving from one country to another is a huge challenge. Just think of driving: in the UK and South Africa we drive on the left side of the road, in Canada and America, on the right side. The steering wheel is on different sides of the car, which is always confusing: why can't it just be in the middle?

In America "pants" are what men and women wear; in England we call them "trousers," and generally "pants" refer to women's frilly underwear! Even though all these countries speak English, when we move from one to another, we sometimes wonder if they speak a foreign language.

One way to adjust to a new culture and country is to "do as the Romans do"—that is, to watch your neighbors and copy what they do. Israel had so much to learn, such as how to farm in a country that was not at all like Egypt. They had to learn how to build houses and develop towns, how to practice law, how to worship God regularly in the land, and so forth. For all the excitement of being in the land, the many, many challenges were daunting, and a real temptation was to copy the example of the Canaanites. Israel had conquered the land, but there were still many Canaanites scattered around the land, and they knew how to farm, where to find water, how to travel from one place to another, and more. What harm could there be in following their example?

Especially in America we tend to think of church (religion) and state as separate. In the world Israel was a part of, every aspect of life was bound up with religion. If you were a Canaanite, for example, you might try and guarantee the fertility of the land and thus successful crops in the coming year by going to the local temple and having sex with a temple prostitute as an act of worship. This broke a whole variety of God's rules for Israel, and so it was essential that in most ways the people not copy the Canaanites, lest they slip into following the Canaanite gods.

Alas—and with Israel's track record you may not be surprised—the period following Israel's conquest of the land was not a good time for her. Time after time, region after region fell to the very temptation we referred to above, adopting Canaanite lifestyles and being drawn into worshiping other gods, just as God had warned them not to do (Exodus 23:23-24). Of course, this was intolerable to God and it broke the very rules Israel had agreed to at Mount Sinai. God responded by punishing the tribe or tribes that succumbed to this temptation by handing them over to their local or neighboring enemies, allowing them to be plundered and oppressed. Pain is often a gift that alerts us to the fact that something is wrong, and this was God's intention with his people.

In this way a cycle developed among the Israelites. First, they drifted away from God and started worshiping the gods of the Canaanites. Then God would punish them. After a while—as they did when they were in Egypt—the oppression would become too much and the Israelites would cry out to God for deliverance. God would hear and then he would raise up a military deliverer to rescue them from their enemies. All would be well for a while . . . and then this terrible cycle would set in again. We can illustrate this cycle as in figure 12.1.

The problem with a dysfunctional relationship is that what is abnormal starts to become normal. As one reads through the book of Judges—named after the military deliverers, who are called *judges*—the cycle of descent into rebellion against God starts to become predictable. But, of course, with God in their midst, it is unsustainable.

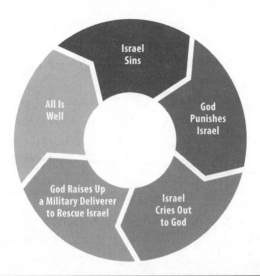

Figure 12.1. The cycle of sin and deliverance

The result is that even as the cycle continues, Israel starts to spiral down into a really bad place, and Israel's military deliverers start looking more and more like Israel herself.

The final judge, Samson, exemplifies this development, showing many of the worst traits of Israel herself. Samson was born by God's intervention and grace to a woman who had been unable to bear children. Samson is consecrated as a "Nazirite," someone set apart from birth to serve God. As a sign of this, the Nazirite was to follow certain practices, such as refraining from strong drink and not cutting his hair. God intends that Samson, as a judge, will deliver the Israelites from one of their major enemies, the Philistines. Samson does indeed deliver Israel from the Philistines, but his lifestyle is far from what we might expect of a judge called by God. He takes a Philistine wife, who would bring her gods with her into the marriage, and cavorts with prostitutes —both expressly prohibited by God. His denial of God's laws, however, leads to an interesting end.

Samson takes another wife, Delilah, and reveals to her the secret of the great strength he has become known for: his uncut hair. One night while he is sleeping, Delilah cuts his hair, allowing for his capture by the Philistines. The end comes as his hair and strength return. At a great festival to the Philistine god Dagon, Samson pulls down the two middle pillars of the building they are all in, killing the Philistine leaders, many other Philistines, and even himself.

God is patient and slow to become angry but not endlessly so. The Philistines remained a thorn in Israel's side, and the Israelites continued to slide down into worshiping other gods. Eventually God allowed the Philistines to defeat the Israelites and—catastrophically—to capture the Ark of the Covenant, the central part of the tabernacle. This was truly disastrous. God's presence among his people made them who they were. But God's house was now positioned amid Israel's enemies. Had Israel drifted so far from God that she was in danger of becoming God's enemy?

At the end of the book of Judges we find a refrain: there was no king in Israel, and everyone did what was right in their own eyes. In other words, the situation had descended into chaos. Was this the end? Where would help come from?

READINGS: Judges 2:11-23 and 1 Samuel 4:1-11

13

A KING LIKE THE OTHER NATIONS?

OUR TELEVISIONS AND NEWS FEEDS constantly confront us with things going wrong in our countries. As we watch such reports, our almost immediate response is to blame our politicians or to look to them alone to solve the problems. Good political leadership is vitally important but so, too, are other types of leadership: the leadership of parents in the home, teachers and principals of schools, coaches of sports teams, church pastors, and so forth. We make a mistake when we put all our hopes in political leadership to ensure we flourish. Sadly, this became a very real temptation for the Israelites as they struggled to break the downward spiral of the period of the judges.

By the time we reach Samson and the end of the period of the military deliverers—the judges—it is as though God's great plans for

Israel have run aground. Israel has spiraled down into chaos, and it's unclear where hope might come from. Even Israel's worship has been contaminated. At this time Eli and his two sons presided as priests over Israel's worship. As we saw in chapter ten when God's portable home was set up, the priests played a vital role in mediating between the holy God and the Israelites. But even here, in God's very presence, Eli's sons had become corrupt and thus their role as mediators was badly damaged: "This sin of the young men was very great in the LORD's sight, for they were treating the LORD's offering with contempt" (1 Samuel 2:17).

Once more God brings hope from an unlikely source. In the ancient world it was a great social stigma for a woman to be barren, and Israel had become like a barren woman, seemingly unable to produce life and goodness and obedience. But Israel's God is able to bring new life out of death, hope out of despair, and a doorway of hope out of the wall of rebellion and defeat. It is thus highly symbolic that the man who would help Israel find a way forward out of her current impasse was born to a barren woman named Hannah.

God heard Hannah's cry for children, and she bore a son named Samuel who, like Samson, was dedicated to God as a Nazirite. Hannah took this dedication of Samuel seriously, and once Samuel was weaned, she handed him over to Eli so that he could grow up—literally—in the presence of God: "And the LORD was gracious to Hannah; she gave birth to three sons and two daughters. Meanwhile, the boy Samuel grew up in the presence of the LORD" (2 Samuel 2:21).

Samuel turned out to be the opposite of Eli's sons. He developed into a faithful priest, and one night he received a message from the Lord that

God would punish Eli's sons. He had the thankless task of conveying this to Eli, but since then he also became known as a *prophet*—namely, one who receives God's messages for God's people. The Philistines attacked the Israelites, as referred to in the previous chapter, and during this battle Eli's corrupt sons were killed. And far more seriously, the Philistines captured the ark from the portable sanctuary.

If this was tragic for Israel, it also turned out to be far more than the Philistines could handle. As was typical in those days, the Philistines thought they would simply add Israel's God to the temple of their god, Dagon. They brought the ark to Ashdod, one of their major cities, and placed it in the temple of Dagon next to Dagon's statue. The next day they found Dagon on his face before the ark. They put him back up again, but the next day he was down again with his head and arms severed clean off. Not surprisingly, the Philistines became terrified and quickly moved the ark to another of their major cities, Gath. But there, disease broke out among the inhabitants, and so it was sent on to another major Philistine city, Ekron, all the time getting closer to Israel. In desperation the Philistines loaded it into a cart and let the cows take it wherever they wished. One can only imagine their amazement when the cows took it back to Israel to the town of Beth Shemesh. From there it was taken north to Kiriath Jearim, where a man named Eleazar was made a priest to care for the ark.

Samuel was a priest and a prophet and also a great military deliverer. He delivered the Israelites from the Philistines and for years traveled from city to city administering justice among the Israelites. Alas, one would have hoped that Samuel learned from the bad parental example of Eli, but Samuel's sons also turned out to be corrupt. Fearing what would happen once Samuel died, the leaders of Israel thought they knew the solution. They came to Samuel and requested that he appoint over them a king, just like the other nations.

These leaders of Israel were like many of us in looking to politics to solve all our problems. But it is a fatal mistake. Israel's problem was not that she didn't have a king like the other nations but that she was not keeping the rules of the great King she did have!

Israel's experience in Egypt, for example, should have alerted her unequivocally to the dangers of monarchy. In Egypt the king was thought to be a god, and he exercised his rule absolutely. Samuel is immediately aware of the dangers in the Israelites' request and alerts them to the fact that a king will require an army and many servants; they will become captive to him. But the leaders will have none of it; they want a king, "like all the other nations." Samuel takes their request to God, and, surprisingly, God tells Samuel to give them a king.

Thus ends the period of the judges, and the period of Israel under the rule of kings begins. It is important to note that God chooses Israel's king.

Following God's instructions, Samuel meets privately with a man of the tribe of Benjamin named Saul and anoints him as king, and then later at a gathering of the people at Mizpah, Saul is chosen by lot to be king.

Saul, however, is a reluctant king. He hides away among the baggage and has to be found and brought forth to be anointed as king. Saul is effective in routing Israel's enemies, and this wins him the support of the people. But in his farewell address to the people, Samuel, as the last judge, rehearses the history of Israel and reminds them that if they and their king live according to God's rules, it will go well with them, but if they rebel against God, they and their king will be swept away.

Alas, it soon becomes apparent that Saul is a mixed bag when it comes to obeying Israel's true King. Saul shows himself impatient in battle and fails to attend closely to God's commands first. As a result, Samuel tells Saul that God has rejected him and that his descendents will not be established as a dynasty. As we soon see, God already has someone else in mind to be king after Saul's reign ends.

In many ways Saul is a tragic figure: impulsive, rash, and impetuous. Although he starts well, the decline sets in early during his reign. Quietly Samuel seeks out God's choice to replace Saul as king. He finds it will be David, "a man after God's own heart." Saul's decline is matched by David's rise. David comes to public recognition when he defeats the Philistine's champion fighter Goliath with a sling and stones, and soon King Saul's devout son Jonathan becomes David's best friend. Saul becomes insanely jealous of David's rise, so—like Cain—he tries to kill him on several occasions. David, though, holds back when he himself could take Saul's life.

By the end of Saul's life, the Philistines remain a major military threat. Saul recognizes he desperately needs to hear from God, but the heavens are now silent. In desperation he goes against God's rules and consults a medium, or a witch. This is such an affront to God that, astonishingly, Samuel returns from beyond the grave to tell Saul that Israel will be defeated by the Philistines and he and his sons will die. And so it is; Saul's sons are killed in battle and, seeing things going badly, Saul literally falls upon his sword, committing suicide.

Clearly, by itself kingship will not save Israel.

READINGS: 1 Samuel 8 and 17

14

A KING AFTER GOD'S OWN HEART?

I T CANNOT BE EASY being heir apparent to the throne. One thinks, for example, of Prince Charles. All his life (now for over seventy years) he has known and had it reinforced daily that he is destined to be king. But what's he to do until that time arrives? David found himself in a similar position. He was anointed king by Samuel relatively early in Saul's reign because of Saul's disobedience. When Samuel saw one of David's brothers, he was so impressive that Samuel thought, *This must be the one!* But God reminded him that humans look on the outside while God looks at the heart, the innermost part of a person. David was the youngest of eight brothers, but he was the one God instructed Samuel to anoint as king.

However, it was one thing being privately anointed by Samuel as king and quite another to actually become the king. In practice and in public

Saul remained king, and for many years after being anointed, David had his hands full negotiating life around Saul's developing madness. Yet once David was anointed, the Spirit of God came upon him, even as it departed from Saul, and it was simply impossible for David to remain quietly in the shadows. David visibly shot to fame like a meteor in the sky when he defeated Goliath, the Philistine's champion fighter, with the most basic of weapons, a sling and stones. Saul did not even know who he was, but as David became a successful military leader and then head of the army, the Israelites composed a new song (see 1 Samuel 18:7):

Saul has slain his thousands,
And David his tens of thousands.

Such songs were not at all to Saul's liking. David's rise called forth Saul's manic jealousy. David was not only a great warrior but also a fine musician, and Saul's first attempt on David's life came when David was playing the lyre for him. Twice Saul tried to pin David to the wall with a spear. But David was greatly loved and not least by members of Saul's own family. Jonathan, one of Saul's sons, was David's best friend, and despite Saul's attempts to have the Philistines kill David in battle, David won the hand of Saul's daughter Michal in marriage.

As you can well imagine, when Saul committed suicide in battle against the Philistines, he left Israel in a political quagmire with a variety of people trying to grab power. David was anointed king publicly over Judah, the southern part of Israel. But Abner, the commander of Saul's army, took Ish-Bosheth, one of Saul's sons, and made him king over the northern part of Israel. It was only some seven years later that David was crowned king over all Israel.

All this brings us to the point when David moves to establish a capital city for the country. David and his troops take possession of the stronghold of Zion—known best as Jerusalem—which later comes to be referred to as "the city of David." David has a palace built for himself on Mount Zion and then sets about bringing the ark to Jerusalem. This is a huge moment for Israel, and the journey of the ark to Jerusalem is accompanied with great fanfare and celebration with King David himself "leaping and dancing before the LORD" (2 Samuel 6:16).

The ark is now at rest in the heart of Israel, and David is keen to build a temple for God to house the ark. But through the prophet Nathan, God tells David that he is not to do this. God reveals that he is establishing David's line as a dynasty but that his successor will build the temple, not David. This agreement with David is known as the covenant with David, summed up in God's promise to David that "your house and your kingdom will endure forever before me; your throne will be established forever" (2 Samuel 7:16). Each of the kings that  followed him in his lineage are known as "the son of David." With God's help, David is extremely successful in defeating Israel's enemies and expanding her territory. David is very different from Saul, and after long years of waiting for David to become king, it seems that all was now well. The country is united, the ark—symbolizing God's presence—is in Jerusalem, as is David's royal palace.

However, as Samuel had warned, kingship was an institution fraught with dangers. Money, sex, and power are the great temptations, and David proved vulnerable to these too.

For some reason, one year when David's troops went out to battle, he remained at home in his palace. One afternoon David was on the roof of his palace surveying the surroundings, and he spotted a very beautiful woman named Bathsheba taking a bath on a nearby rooftop. David inquired about her and learned that she was married to Uriah the Hittite. But a king is all-powerful, right? Knowing that she was married did not stop David. He had her brought to him so he could have sex with her. Some weeks later he received a worrying message from Bathsheba: "I am pregnant."

Events were now set in motion that would lead to the worst aspects of King David's reign. To conceal what had transpired, David had Bathsheba's husband, Uriah, recalled from battle, in the hope that he would sleep with his wife and so assume the child was his. But Uriah had integrity, and like a good commander, he refused to enjoy the pleasures of home while his troops were out in the field. David then had Uriah return to his troops and arranged for his military commander Joab to have Uriah positioned in battle so that he was killed. Adultery had now led to murder. After a suitable time of mourning had passed, David took Bathsheba as his wife. She gave birth to a son, but the son, conceived in such terrible circumstances, died.

Murder and adultery are abhorrent to God; they are clearly forbidden in the Ten Commandments. God responds by sending Nathan the prophet to tell David a story. It is a story of a city in which a poor man and a rich man lived. The rich man had many flocks whereas all the poor man had was a lamb. The lamb grew up with the poor man's children and became like a member of the family—as we would say, a much-loved pet. The rich man had a guest, and rather than slaughter one of his flock, he took the poor man's lamb and served it up for his guest. David is apoplectic when he hears this and declares that the rich man deserves the death penalty. Nathan replies, "You are the man!"

Nathan tells him that because of what he has done, God will stir up trouble within his royal household. David realizes what he has done and cries out to God for forgiveness. Psalm 51 is thought to be a prayer of repentance that David composed at this time. It begins,

Have mercy on me, O God,
    according to your unfailing love;
according to your great compassion
    blot out my transgressions.
Wash away all my iniquity
    and cleanse me from my sin.
For I know my transgressions,
    and my sin is always before me.
Against you, you only, have I sinned
    and done what is evil in your sight;
so you are right in your verdict
    and justified when you judge. (Psalm 51:1-4)

Nathan assures David that God has forgiven his sin. The consequences of the sin still remain, however, and sometime later one of David's sons, Absalom, conspires against him and seeks to take over the throne from David. Things get so bad that David has to flee Jerusalem and is only able to return after the assassination of Absalom by David's troops.

In so many ways David was a great king. Many of the hymns in the book of Psalms come from him, and they reveal him to be a man of deep devotion to God. But his fall into adultery and then murder was inexcusable, and it triggered events that overshadowed his final years, nearly toppling him as king. Bathsheba bore him another son, Solomon, after their first child died, and Solomon succeeded David as king.

READINGS: 2 Samuel 7 and Psalm 51

15

A WISE KING?

FEW OF US WOULD HAVE WANTED to be the leader of a country when the coronavirus struck. It spread like wildfire, was deadly, and seemed unstoppable. Our global, connected world created routes for the virus to move astonishingly quickly across the planet. Governments needed to assess the threat and get appropriate rules in place fast. Some dismissed the threat and were slow to respond. Others saw the seriousness of the virus quickly and rapidly got measures in place to protect their populations. This is what the Bible calls "wisdom" (see Proverbs 1:1-7). King David's son and successor, King Solomon, became famous for his wisdom.

After David's death, it takes a while for Solomon to consolidate his position as king over Israel. David had urged Solomon to obey God so that his reign would be successful, and at a certain point early in his reign Solomon goes to Gibeon to worship God. There God appears to him in a dream with a dazzling offer: "Ask for whatever you want me to give you." What might we have asked for if we were in Solomon's shoes? Solomon responds with real humility, telling God that he is young and terribly inadequate for the task now fallen to him. He thus asks God, "Give your servant a discerning heart to govern your people and to distinguish between right and wrong. For who is able to govern this great people of yours?" (1 Kings 3:9).

God is delighted with Solomon's request and responds accordingly: "I will do what you have asked. I will give you a wise and discerning heart,

so that there will never have been anyone like you, nor will there ever be" (1 Kings 3:11). God promises to give him also what he has not asked for— namely, wealth and honor. If Solomon obeys God, God will grant him a full, long life.

Solomon does indeed receive great wisdom, for which he becomes renowned. Wisdom includes knowledge, and Solomon becomes an expert on trees, animals, birds, reptiles, and fish. In today's terms we might say he became the leading natural scientist of his day. But wisdom is about more than knowledge.

Doubtless you have heard jokes about academics, beginning, for example, "How many academics does it take to change a light bulb?"

We can have a great deal of knowledge about a small area of life but be quite useless when it comes to practical issues like changing a light bulb or fixing a tap or, more importantly, knowing how to cope with the challenges of life. Solomon had a great deal of theoretical knowledge, but he also possessed practical wisdom. Solomon wrote many pithy proverbs, an attempt to encapsulate wisdom in short, brief, memorable sayings. The contemporary expression "He who laughs last laughs the loudest" is a proverb in this sense. Many of Solomon's proverbs are found in the Old Testament book by this name, Proverbs.

As king, Solomon certainly needed wisdom, and he became famous for his wise judgments. For example, as king he would sometimes be asked to adjudicate in particularly difficult cases. Once two prostitutes came to him. Both had borne sons, but one of the sons had died, and both now claimed that the living son was theirs (1 Kings 3:16-28). What to do? One of the women was lying, but which one? Audaciously, Solomon called for a sword and then said, "Divide the child into two and give half to each woman!" The real mother immediately reacted, saying, "Let the other woman have the child," rather than have her son killed. Thus the real mother was revealed, the case solved, and justice was seen to be done.

Solomon increased the administration of Israel, extended the kingdom of Israel, and acquired great wealth. But his greatest achievement was to build a permanent house for God in Jerusalem, the temple. You can see the design of the temple in figure 15.1. In many ways the temple was a continuation of the portable tabernacle: both were God's royal residence amid his people. However, there were also important differences.

Whereas the tabernacle was temporary, suitable for journeying and settling in the land, the temple was permanent, suitable for a time

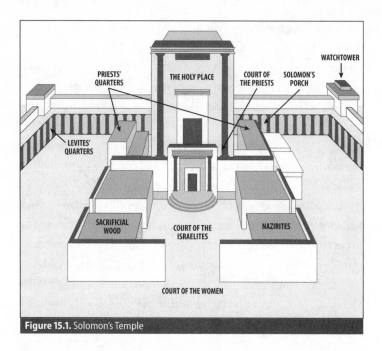

Figure 15.1. Solomon's Temple

when Israel was settled in the land and had rest from all her enemies. The temple had similar rooms to the tabernacle, but it was much bigger. Like the tabernacle, every room was highly symbolic. The building, as you can see from the image, was built in a pyramid shape like a holy mountain. The tabernacle was like a portable Mount Sinai; in this way, and in many others, the mountain-shaped temple evoked Israel's history. The interior of the temple was covered with cedar wood from Lebanon, and the walls had fruit, flowers, and vegetables carved into them, recalling the Garden of Eden. Angelic figures called cherubim guarded the entrance to the inner sanctuary—the holy of holies, or most holy place, where God's throne was located—just as cherubim guarded the entrance to Eden once Adam and Eve were exiled from it. Eden was well watered (Genesis 2), and the temple contained much water. A large basin called the "Sea of cast metal" was constructed, probably symbolizing the restless sea of the Gentile nations of the world. Ten water stands were made, evoking water flowing out of the temple. The temple was awash with gold, while bronze was used for the less holy parts. In all these and other ways, the temple evoked for Israel the long journey of which she was a central part. Her ancestors were cast out of Eden for their rebellion, but here God was planting his people in a land with him as their resident King, as though Eden had been recovered.

Amid huge festivities lasting seven days, the temple was dedicated and the ark brought into the holy of holies. Once the priests placed the ark in the holy of holies, God's glory filled the temple. God assured Solomon that he was present amid his people, living in his palace, the temple. As has been said, God now had an address on earth! However, his presence was never automatic and could never be taken for granted. It remained conditional on his people obeying him and keeping the covenant, the agreement between God and Israel.

Solomon was very gifted and his achievements, momentous; he expanded Israel's territory, developed an extensive royal administration, built a fleet of ships, and more. But alas, he had serious faults. If David fell afoul of sex, Solomon succumbed to money, power, *and* sex. He was a political strategist par excellence, and even before God gave him the gift of wisdom, he took one of Pharaoh's daughters as one of his many wives to establish a political alliance with Egypt. He had hundreds of wives in his harem, many of them foreign, bringing with them worship of foreign gods. With time this affected Solomon, bending his heart away from God and encouraging him and his people to break the first commandment: You shall have no other gods besides me.

As with David, God became angry with Solomon. He allowed unrest to develop in the kingdom, with usurpers arising to challenge Solomon's authority. All Solomon's projects had taken a heavy toll on the Israelites—they bore the brunt of the work involved, just as Samuel had warned (see 1 Samuel 8:10-18)—and they became susceptible to the lure of alternative leadership as the charm of kingship wore thin.

The building of the temple and its consecration, however, was a remarkable moment in Israel's history. It was as though God and the Israelites—remember, they were formerly enslaved and brutally oppressed—had finally come home. Surely now Israel could move forward to fulfill its potential as God's chosen people with the living God in their midst. Surely they could now live so that the other nations could see in them what life looked like as God intended it to be.

The temple—God's royal residence in their midst—was the glue that held the Israelites together. It was, among other things, the great symbol of their unity as one people in one land under the rule of the one God. Sadly, with Solomon's death his reign's toll on the people erupted like a dam bursting, and Israel split into two kingdoms under two different kings. Unintentionally, Solomon's ambition paved the way for this catastrophic split of Israel into the Southern Kingdom and the Northern Kingdom. After Solomon's death, Jeroboam became leader of the ten tribes of the Northern Kingdom and Solomon's son, Rehoboam, king of the two tribes of the Southern Kingdom. These were ominous developments.

READINGS: 1 Kings 3 and 8:1-21

THE NORTHERN KINGDOM

Israel

A SPLIT BETWEEN people, communities, or countries is difficult. We see the effects of this in our daily lives; we also see what happens in the modern world as countries attempt to separate or when relationships break down. The separation does not just affect the parties involved but countless people around them. That's why God seeks the good of the whole: the pain of separation does not allow for the fullness of life God intended. Instead, it brings suffering and tears.

God is the glue that holds his people together, so long as people do not turn away from him. If they turn their back on him, the consequences are catastrophic, as we will soon see.

King Jeroboam, king of the Northern Kingdom, was immediately aware of the challenge Jerusalem and God's house there presented to him as king (1 Kings 12:25-33). If his people went south to worship God in Jerusalem, the Northern Kingdom would soon revert to being part of Israel as a whole, and he would lose his realm. On no account could he allow this to happen. He decided that religion, rather than serving God, must be made to serve the state—that is, himself. After all, such a model seemed to work well enough in the surrounding nations. And so, just like the Israelites who grew impatient when Moses was delayed on Mount Sinai with God, Jeroboam decided to act before the issue of where to worship God became a problem.

So Jeroboam had two calves of gold forged and said to the northern Israelites, "You have been going down to Jerusalem to worship God for long enough. Forget Jerusalem. Here are your gods who brought you out of Egypt." He set one of the calves in Bethel and one in Dan, at the southern and northern extremities of his kingdom, and established centers for worship there.

This was a complete violation of God's covenant with Israel as set out in the first two of the Ten Commandments: "You shall have no other gods before me" and "You shall not make for yourself an image in the form of anything in heaven above or on the earth beneath or in the waters below. You shall not bow down to them or worship them" (Deuteronomy 5:7-9). This set the Northern Kingdom on a downward spiral, and not surprisingly, as the stories of the northern kings are told, we hear again and again of king after king who "did evil in the eyes of the LORD."

King Ahab's reign was a particularly low point in the history of the Northern Kingdom. Ahab married a foreign woman, Jezebel, and actively worshiped the god of her people, Baal. Baal was a Canaanite god believed by his followers to provide rain, fertility, fire, and lightning and to guarantee good crops. How would God respond to this blatant provocation? A major way was through his spokespeople, the prophets.

In the story thus far, we have encountered *prophets,* men—and in some cases women—to whom God conveys his message so that they can convey it to his people. In the Old Testament, for example, Moses is the greatest prophet. With God's direction, he not only leads the people out of slavery into the Promised Land but provides them with rules for living that will enable them to live life to the fullest.

As kingship develops in Israel, prophets start to play a major role as God's counterbalance to the power of the king. A danger with kingship, as we have already seen, is that the king starts to view his power as absolute and forgets that above all else he is called to live under God's reign and to help his people to do the same. We saw, for example, how the prophet Nathan confronted David after David committed adultery and murder. God demonstrates his patience, in part, by calling individuals to be prophets, to speak his truth to power and often to enact before both king and people that only Yahweh is truly God.

As Ahab embraces idolatry, God raises up a prophet named Elijah to confront him. One can only imagine the courage it must have taken to be called to such a job! Jezebel takes delight in having God's prophets murdered, so this is serious business. Again and again Elijah's confrontation with Ahab demonstrates that the power Ahab and Jezebel ascribe to the pagan god Baal belongs instead only to Israel's God—it is God who sends the rain to irrigate the ground, not Baal. But Ahab remains unmoved. Consequently, Elijah informs Ahab of what God has told him: there will be no rain for three years. Famine hits the Northern Kingdom. Only when Elijah informs Ahab that God says rain will come is the famine broken. Still Ahab remains devoted to Baal worship.

Baal is also thought to be the god of lightning and fire. So Elijah issues Ahab a challenge. Eight hundred of the prophets of Ahab's gods should assemble on Mount Carmel, as well as the people of Israel. Elijah has two bulls slaughtered and two altars erected with a bull on each one. Ahab's prophets are to call on their gods to send fire and consume their sacrifice. Elijah will call on the God of Israel. The God who answers by fire will be shown to be the true God. Ahab's prophets cry out to their gods and cut themselves so that their blood runs out, as was their practice. "But there was no response, no one answered, no one paid attention" (1 Kings 18:29).

By evening Elijah has prepared his altar and has it soaked with water, so that if it catches fire, there could be no other explanation than God's intervention. He prays to God saying, "Answer me, LORD, answer me,

so these people will know that you, LORD, are God, and that you are turning their hearts back again" (1 Kings 18:37). Fire falls from the heavens, consuming the sacrifice, the wood, the stones, the dust, and even all the water. One would think that this remarkable demonstration of the living God would persuade Ahab and Jezebel, but quite the reverse happens. It hardens their hearts.

What we worship shapes the way we live, and so it continued to be with Ahab and Jezebel. The valley of

Jezreel is one of the most fertile places in Israel, and Ahab spots a vineyard there, owned by Naboth, that he decides he wants. But Naboth declines to sell his ancestral property, so Ahab and Jezebel conspire to have Naboth falsely accused and stoned to death. God's patience is running out. Through Elijah, God tells Ahab that he and Jezebel will themselves suffer terrible deaths. Sometime later Ahab is killed in battle. Later Jezebel is thrown to her death from the upper story of a house (2 Kings 9:30-37).

In his patience God continues to send other prophets to the Northern Kingdom to turn their hearts back to him: Elijah is, for example, succeeded by another feisty prophet, Elisha. Another prophet, Amos, is a farmer in the Southern Kingdom but is called to prophesy to the Northern Kingdom in particular. Amos is a masterly preacher. For example, he preaches a sermon steadily going round the Northern Kingdom's neighbors and declaring God's judgment on them. He uses the terrifying image of God as a lion roaring, something lions do to paralyze their prey with fear as they are about to pounce on it. One can just imagine the crowds cheering as Israel's neighbors, Damascus, Gaza, Ekron, Tyre, and others, are called out for their sins and condemned. But slowly the noose tightens as Amos turns his focus to Israel.

Amos first declares God's judgment on the Southern Kingdom, Judah. And then . . . he unleashes God's coming punishment on the Northern Kingdom. Amos declares that the Northern Kingdom, called Israel, is condemned for human rights violations, for terrible immorality, and perverse religiosity. The coming punishment comes to be represented by a phrase that starts to crop up in Amos and in the words of the other prophets: "that day" or "the day of the LORD."

This is a day or time when punishment is coming if the Northern Kingdom does not change its ways.

And, alas, it does not change. As a small nation sandwiched between Egypt and the great empires of Mesopotamia, Israel is always vulnerable. God alone can enable her to survive and flourish. Assyria has emerged as the great empire of the day, and she soon casts her eye on Israel. God's patience has expired, and he allows the Assyrians to conquer the Northern Kingdom and to take them off into exile in Assyria in 722 BC. Will the Southern Kingdom learn from her example?

READINGS: 1 Kings 18:16-40 and 2 Kings 17:1-18

THE SOUTHERN KINGDOM

Judah

SOMETIMES PEOPLE use religion as a kind of magic charm to ward off bad things from happening to them. That's what people do in the *Godfather* films about mafia leaders and their families. These men commit the most terrible murders and robberies but are devout men who care for their families, attend mass, and donate to the church. They believe or hope that their religion will protect them from God's punishment despite how they live.

This was the great danger of the Southern Kingdom, Judah. In chapter fifteen we mentioned that God's house, his royal palace, was in the Southern Kingdom, in Jerusalem. It was hard for southerners to imagine that God would allow anything really bad to happen to Judah as long as his house (the temple) was present in their midst.

Were their kings not sons of David, and had not God promised to establish David's dynasty forever?

Tragically, the southerners failed to see that privilege and responsibility go hand in hand. The privilege of having God in your midst brings great responsibility. Instead the southerners began to take God for granted, much like many do today. They were devout members of their church but lived lives that didn't match biblical teachings. "Go to the temple for worship to keep God happy but live as you like" was the motto of far too many of them.

Once again God was patient with his people. He sent a series of prophets to them to call them to change their ways, to turn back to him, and to obey him, and then he would indeed look after them. The sayings of many of

these prophets were recorded and preserved for future reference and eventually became part of the Bible. Again and again the prophets proclaimed to anyone who will listen, "Thus says the LORD."

One of these remarkable individuals was Jeremiah; the collection of his prophecies is named after him. Jeremiah was called to be a prophet around 626 BC, during the reign of King Josiah of the Southern Kingdom, and he continued his ministry until after the capture of Jerusalem by the Babylonians in 587 BC. This means that he lived and prophesied during a critical time in the life of God's people. In his book we also find several of his prayers, prayers that reveal just how agonizing it was to be a prophet at a time like this. Jeremiah was frequently overwhelmed by his task and the dangerous complacency that had taken hold in the south. In one of his prayers he cried out,

> Alas, my mother, that you gave me birth,
>> a man with whom the whole land strives and contends!
> I have neither lent nor borrowed,
>> yet everyone curses me. (Jeremiah 15:10)

Jeremiah had to dig deep in his relationship with God to find the strength for his challenging mission. Like the other prophets, Jeremiah used every rhetorical strategy and enactment of his message to try and rouse the southerners out of their complacency. It was not that the citizens of Judah were unreligious—they flocked to the temple in Jerusalem—but their lives contradicted their worship.

God knew only too well the hearts of the southerners, and one day he gave Jeremiah an unenviable mission. Jeremiah was told to stand at the gate to the temple as the citizens of Judah flocked in to "worship" and to prophesy:

> Hear the word of the LORD, all you people of Judah who come through these gates to worship the LORD. This is what the LORD Almighty, the God of Israel, says: Reform your ways and your actions, and I will let you live in this place. Do not trust in deceptive words and say, "This is the temple of the LORD, the temple of the LORD, the temple of the LORD!" If you really

change your ways and your actions and deal with each other
justly, if you do not oppress the foreigner, the fatherless or the
widow and do not shed innocent blood in this place, and if you
do not follow other gods to your own harm, then I will let you
live in this place, in the land I gave your ancestors for ever and
ever. But look, you are trusting in deceptive words that are
worthless. (Jeremiah 7:2-8)

Jeremiah nailed it. He put his finger right on the problem with the people
of Judah. Despite their disobedient lives, they were trusting that because
the temple stood in Jerusalem, God would never let judgment come upon
them. Later in this sermon, God warned the Israelites through Jeremiah
that if they did not change their ways, he would do the unimaginable: he
would destroy them and the temple. You can just imagine how unpopular
such a message was. Prophets like Jeremiah suffered and were persecuted
as they spoke the truth to the people of Judah.

Unlike the Northern Kingdom, the Southern Kingdom after
Solomon had some good kings in the line of David who sought to
reform her and bring her back to God. For example, it is said of kings
Amaziah (c. 800–783 BC), Azariah (c. 791–739 BC), and Jotham
(c. 742–735 BC) that they did what was right in the eyes of God. But it
is also noted that they did not eradicate the many "high places" where
other gods were worshiped in Judah. King Ahaz (c. 732–716 BC), by
contrast, actively participated in the false worship at the high places,
and then, when Judah was under threat from her enemies, he took
silver and gold from the temple and sent it to the King of Assyria in
exchange for his help. It is not hard to see how from God's point of
view this was treason.

Amazingly one good southern king ascended to the throne as a young child, Jehoash (c. 835–796 BC). Jehoash was taught God's instruction by the priests, and he made a concerted effort to call Judah back to obedience to God. So, too, did King Hezekiah (c. 715–686 BC) and King Josiah (c. 640–610 BC), but at this stage, time was running out for Judah. During Josiah's reign the book of the law (probably Deuteronomy) was found in the temple, and Josiah initiated a major reform after having it read to the people.

By now Babylon had replaced Assyria as the superpower of the day, and Babylon was breathing down Judah's neck as she expanded her empire. Tragically, Josiah was replaced by an evil king, King Jehoahaz (c. 605–598 BC), and his reign triggered God's punishment. The Southern Kingdom of Judah was conquered by Babylon, the people of Judah were taken off into exile in Babylon in 597 and again in 587 BC, and in 587 BC the temple was destroyed.

We can hardly imagine what it must have felt like to be marched off as prisoners into exile in Babylon with the temple ransacked and destroyed. What had gone so terribly wrong? Where was God in all this? Was this the end of God's promise to Abraham and his descendents? It must have been very easy to reach this conclusion. But God continued to speak to his people through his prophets, and this saved the day. The prophets continued to prophesy, and prophets like Jeremiah went with the people into exile. Ezekiel prophesied in Babylon (c. 592–570 BC).

The Israelites had to discover that God was bigger than their land and the temple. He is the Lord of heaven and earth and cannot be confined to a land, a nation, or a temple. Even as the prophets explained that God's judgment had come upon his people because of their sustained rebellion and disobedience, the prophets looked forward.

This was not the end. God remained committed to his purposes, and these prophets began to speak of a messiah, a true son of David, who would come and rescue his people, cleanse them from their sins, and inaugurate a new covenant between God and his people (for example, Jeremiah 31:31-34).

READINGS: 2 Kings 24–25 and Jeremiah 7:1-15

EXILE AND RETURN

NOWADAYS WE KNOW about exiles. Thousands of refugees and immigrants have been making their way to Europe and North America in recent years. How hard life must be for refugees! They are forced to flee from their homeland, desperately hoping to find refuge and welcome in a new land. One of our friends works as a counselor for refugees, and she describes just how difficult the experience is for them. It is an agonizing time of loss and fear and then often of repeated rejection and despair.

At least if you are fleeing, there is the fragile hope of finding a refuge. But most of the citizens of the Southern Kingdom were dragged off to exile in Babylon as prisoners and forced to settle there. And to make the situation much worse, they had brought this punishment upon themselves. Psalm 137 was written in this tragic context. It laments the destruction of Jerusalem and captures well the pathos of exile:

By the rivers of Babylon we sat and wept
     when we remembered Zion.
There on the poplars
     we hung our harps,
for there our captors asked us for songs,
     our tormentors demanded songs of joy;
     they said, "Sing us one of the songs of Zion!"
How can we sing the songs of the LORD
     while in a foreign land?
If I forget you, Jerusalem,
     may my right hand forget its skill.
May my tongue cling to the roof of my mouth
     if I do not remember you,
if I do not consider Jerusalem
     my highest joy. (Psalm 137:1-6)

Readers may find the words of this psalm familiar. It was turned into a pop song a long time ago. Brent Dowe, lead singer of the Melodians, explained that he adapted Psalm 137 to the new reggae style in "By the Rivers of Babylon" to increase public awareness of the Rastafarian movement and its commitment to black liberation and social justice. The Melodians recorded the song in 1970. A version of it was also released by Bob Marley. In Europe the Boney M cover version in 1978 became one of the top ten all-time bestselling singles ever released in Britain, which is why even today many will have heard some version of this song. Any of us who have experienced pain and rejection can identify with the words of the psalm, but for the Israelites it expressed the loss of "Zion," of God living in their midst in their land.

Where was hope to be found amid this catastrophic experience? One way was through the Israelite exiles expressing their grief before God. Following the book of Jeremiah in the Old Testament is the book Lamentations, a long cry of sorrow about what happened to Jerusalem. As counselors often note, anyone who has been through a deep depression can resonate with much of this book (see, for ex-

ample, Lamentations 3). Indeed, the author of Lamentations works his way toward hope and a prayer for God to restore Israel.

The prophets proved indispensable in moving the people from despair to hope by continuing to speak God's word to his bewildered people. They helped make sense of the exiles' experience, guiding them to realize God was in it with them. There were charlatan prophets around who encouraged the exiles to think that they would quickly be delivered and would return home. We can imagine how attractive this false hope sounded to the exiles. God, however, remarkably and wonderfully, delivered words of true hope and instruction to his desolate people through his genuine prophets.

The prophet Jeremiah, who at this time was still in Jerusalem, sent a letter to the exiles in Babylon telling them from God to "seek the peace and prosperity of the city to which I have carried you into exile. Pray to the LORD for it, because if it prospers, you too will prosper" (Jeremiah 29:7). Jeremiah went on to tell them from God that there would be no quick fix, no quick return from exile. Only after some seventy years would God open the door for them to go back to Israel.

Seventy years sounds like forever when life is tough. And empires like Babylon seem eternal. But in reality, empires come and go. We have seen how Babylon replaced Assyria as the great empire of the day, and the time came when Babylon was defeated by Persia. King Cyrus of Persia had a very different approach to exiles. Some seventy years after the Israelites in Judah had been dragged off into exile, in 522 BC, he decreed that any Israelites who wished could return to Jerusalem. By no means did all of the exiles opt to return, but many did.

Returning was wonderful but also full of challenges. The great priority was to rebuild the temple. Initially the returnees set up the altar and worshiped God there. Then, despite opposition from surrounding groups, they laid the foundations of the new temple and got on with building it. God raised up more prophets such as Haggai (who began to prophesy around 520 BC) and Zechariah (c. 520–518 BC) to encourage them to push on with building the temple despite resistance. Haggai, for example, brought the following message from God:

> "Is it a time for you yourselves to be living in your paneled houses, while this house remains a ruin?" . . .
>
> This is what the LORD Almighty says: "Give careful thought to your ways. Go up into the mountains and bring down timber and build my house, so that I may take pleasure in it and be honored," says the LORD. . . .

Then Zerubbabel son of Shealtiel, Joshua son of Jozadak, the high priest, and the whole remnant of the people obeyed the voice of the LORD their God and the message of the prophet Haggai, because the LORD their God had sent him. And the people feared the LORD.

Then Haggai, the LORD's messenger, gave this message of the LORD to the people: "I am with you," declares the LORD. So the LORD stirred up the spirit of Zerubbabel son of Shealtiel, governor of Judah, and the spirit of Joshua son of Jozadak, the high priest, and the spirit of the whole remnant of the people. They came and began to work on the house of the LORD Almighty, their God, on the twenty-fourth day of the sixth month. (Haggai 1:4, 7-8, 12-15)

If Israel was to survive, rebuilding the temple was not enough, as she knew well from her history. Moses himself had warned God's people that they would not live long in the land if they rebelled against God (Deuteronomy 30:15-18). It was imperative that this time they obey God and live according to his rules. Again God provided. A priest and scholar of God's law, Ezra, returned from exile (c. 458 BC), and he set about leading the people back to God through prayer and repentance and by teaching them God's ways.

So much more remained to be done. In exile in Babylon, one man named Nehemiah had risen to service in the royal palace as cupbearer of the king. His heart broke when he heard of the state of Jerusalem, and after receiving permission to return to Jerusalem (c. 445 BC), he led the challenging task of rebuilding the walls of Jerusalem. Ezra worked alongside him to keep the people's hearts in tune with the physical restoration of Jerusalem.

God's people were back in the land, albeit a much smaller part of it. The temple was rebuilt, as were the walls of Jerusalem, with the worship of God continuing once again on Mount Zion. But it was a shadow of Israel's past glory in the heady days of King David and King Solomon. Soon Israel entered a period of some four hundred years— about the same length of time the Israelites were in Egypt before being rescued by Moses—during which time God's voice through the prophets went silent.

However, records had been kept of the sayings of many of the great prophets, and these prophets spoke of a future day when God would return to his people, vanquish their enemies once and for all, and establish his reign in his world. Such hopes gathered around a promised figure, a son of David, the Messiah, through whom God would achieve his purposes. As we will see, during these four hundred years, the Jews kept this hope alive, with different groups imagining different ways in which God's promises might come to pass.

READINGS: Psalm 137:1-6 and Haggai 1

AN IN-BETWEEN TIME

THE FOUR HUNDRED YEARS or so when God's voice goes silent in Israel is like winter in some countries. So much activity precedes the change of season, but as winter sets in, nature quiets down. Whereas before one might have seen squirrels and chipmunks hurtling around, as they are prone to do, and lots of different species of birds, now all seems silent and forlorn. Some animals go into hibernation, having stored up food in their nests for the long winter. Many birds migrate, flying long distances to warmer places.

It seems as though life is on hold until spring comes. But appearances can be deceiving. Beneath the surface, trees and plants can be busy extending their roots deep into the cold soil. Animals enjoy the rest of hibernation in preparation for the burst of activity in the spring, and so on. Much the same happened with the four hundred years lying between the Old Testament and the New Testament.

As we have seen, the small land of Israel was always in danger of being overshadowed and oppressed by the great empires of the day. Positioned where it is, major trade routes flowed through Israel to the south and to the north. For this and other reasons, any great empire in the ancient Near East had a vested interest in controlling Israel. Now that Israel was reduced to Judea, part of the Southern Kingdom and a shadow of its former greatness, the potential impact of surrounding nations and the empires of the day increased exponentially.

Much of this four-hundred-year period involved Judea in repeated attempts to secure her independence and to wrest control over her affairs away from interfering emperors. As we saw earlier, empires, which at the time seemed eternal, come and go. The same is true during this time. We saw how King Cyrus of Persia was used by God to allow the Jews to return to Jerusalem. Almost two hundred years later, in 330 BC, the later Persian King Darius III and his army were defeated by Alexander the Great, inaugurating the widespread Greek Empire.

One of Alexander's policies was to spread Greek language and culture throughout the empire. Many Jews had not returned to Jerusalem, and as a result, groups of Jews dotted the empire. With Greek now the dominant language, the Jews began in this period the process of translating the whole of the Old Testament into Greek. The translation is known as the Septuagint (from the Latin word for "seventy," based on the legend that it was done by seventy translators). As we will see in the coming chapters, this laid the groundwork in an extraordinary way for what God was soon to do. It may have been winter, but God was doing a lot below the surface, preparing to unveil his amazing plans for the whole world.

In the second century BC some Jews famously revolted against their Greek rulers. But all Jews kept alive God's commandments in one way or another. Worship of the one true God in the ways he commanded was of vital importance to them, and this rubbed Greek authorities the wrong way as they sought to spread and impose Greek culture wherever they could. In 167 BC Greek officials arrived in the town of Modi'in, a town west of Jerusalem, and demanded that the Jews there sacrifice a pig to the Greek gods. The town elder, Mattathias, refused. Such an action would violate everything Jews stood for. But one Jew, deeply influenced by Greek culture, agreed. As he was about to sacrifice the pig, Mattathias stabbed him and the Greek official present. Mattathias then turned to the crowd: "Let every one who is zealous for the law and supports the covenant come out with me!" (1 Maccabees 2:27 NRSV).

Mattathias, his sons, and their followers fled to the hills. There they organized a guerrilla army led by one of Mattathias's sons, Judah, nicknamed "Maccabee," meaning "the hammer." Thus began the Maccabean revolt, which extended over many years. Against all odds the Maccabees were able to regain Jerusalem and to consecrate the temple there. Yet the Greek Empire was followed by the Roman one. In 146 BC the Greeks were defeated by the Romans at the Battle of Corinth. Only in 63 BC did the Romans gain full control of Jerusalem after a century of Israelite independence.

The Romans became famous for their skills in building and not least in building roads that greatly facilitated travel between the countries and cities that constituted their empire. Rome enforced peace across the vast empire in what became known as the Pax Romana, the "peace of Rome." Once again these geopolitical realities laid the ground for what God would do in the future.

As we saw in chapters sixteen and seventeen, the prophets kept hope alive when first the Northern Kingdom and then the Southern Kingdom descended into rebellion and then the judgment of exile. Even as the prophets warned God's people again and again that unless they changed their minds and their lives and lived as they had promised to do, judgment was coming, they also raised Israel's eyes to a time in the future when God would intervene decisively to vanquish his enemies, establish his people, and bring the whole of creation and history under his reign. Sometimes you get the impression from some people that the Bible is all about letting go of this world and heading for heaven as a disembodied soul, as fast as possible! This is simply not the case, as we have seen and will continue to see. The world and history were made by God, and his purpose is to recover what he always intended for them. During the four-hundred-year period, several very different groups developed among the Jews, but all of them, albeit in very different ways, were looking for God's reign to come *in history*.

The major groups that developed in Judaism during this period are the Pharisees, the Sadducees, the Zealots, and the Essenes. The *Pharisees* were a devout religious group—their name comes from a Greek word meaning "to separate"—who were deeply concerned with practicing every aspect of God's law down to the finest detail. Thus they sought to keep themselves separate from others, especially Gentiles, who did not follow these laws. Closely related to this is that they wanted to resist the Greek influence on every aspect of culture that Alexander the Great initiated.

Whereas the Pharisees had much popular appeal and support among the Jews, another group, the *Sadducees*, tended to be more from the upper class. The Sadducees concentrated their attention on the temple and its worship, accepted only the first five books of the Old Testament—the Pentateuch—as God's Word, and denied that when people died they would be resurrected from the dead—a view that, as we will see, the New Testament strongly contradicts.

Although all these groups wished to be free of foreign rule, the *Zealots* had a distinctive handle on how to achieve this. The Zealots were like the freedom fighters of the day, the Maccabees, believing that the Jews needed to get their military act together and repel their foreign overlords by force.

Finally, the *Essenes*, just like the Pharisees, observed the laws of the Old Testament to the letter and believed in immortality but denied the resurrection of the body. Unlike the Pharisees, the Essenes withdrew completely from public life, living in separate communities a bit like monks. Perhaps you have heard of the Dead Sea Scrolls, which contain some of our earliest manuscripts of the Old Testament. Most likely the Essenes produced and preserved these texts, which were discovered in Qumran in Israel in the mid-twentieth century.

All of these groups agreed that their present position under the tyranny of Roman rule was intolerable. All of them had their own ideas about how best to align with God's will so that when God acted, they would be prepared and paying attention.

And then, one day in the first century AD, news began to spread among the Jews. A rather strange man had begun preaching that the time had arrived: God, the great King, was on his way, and his people needed to prepare a path for him, to repent, be cleansed from their many sins, and get ready for his arrival.

In chapter eleven we saw how the Israelites entered the Promised Land from across the Jordan River. This man, whose name was John, went to the same region, preaching that Jews should repent and be baptized—that is, go under the water and come back up again. This in itself was a strange request; baptism was the practice of non-Jews wishing to become Jews. Their baptism was part of the process of becoming a Jew and was a symbol of purification. But telling Jews to be baptized in the Jordan River was not the only thing that made John strange. He ate locusts and wild honey from the desert region where he lived, and his clothes were odd as well. His act of calling Jews to repent and be baptized earned him the name John the Baptist.

John was a fearless preacher, calling people out for their sins no matter who they were. Crowds started to go out to hear him preach, and he developed a significant following. The leaders—namely, the Pharisees, Sadducees, and Zealots—did not know what to make of all of this. John wasn't one of them; how could he take this role upon himself?

The voice of prophecy was back. After a long silence, God was again speaking. Something big was underway.

Act three ("The King Chooses Israel: Salvation Initiated") has been a long one. We are now at the beginning of act four, the central act in the drama of the Bible.

READINGS: Isaiah 40 and Mark 1:1-8

A VOICE CRYING IN
THE WILDERNESS

I N THE GLOBAL SINGING COMPETITION *The Voice*, the judges have their backs to the person singing. In this way a singer is judged entirely on his or her voice and not on his or her appearance. When they turn their chairs around, sometimes the judges see the sort of person they imagined; at other times they're surprised at the appearance of the person connected with the voice they've just heard.

After some four hundred years of silence, God began speaking again in the person of John the Baptist. And just as with judges in *The Voice*, we might be surprised by the appearance of God's newest prophet. His appearance (he wore camel's hair with a belt around his waist) and his diet (he ate locusts and wild honey) were peculiar. He lived in the desert. But what really counted were the words he spoke and where he said them. He was announcing the beginning of act four: "The Coming of the King: Salvation Accomplished." A major description of John is "the voice" (see Mark 1:3 NRSV).

The great time of fulfillment was happening when God would act decisively to achieve his purposes. The writers of the four Gospels at the start of the New Testament (Matthew, Mark, Luke, and John) go out of their way to stress how John the Baptist fulfills the prophecies of the Old Testament. At the outset of his Gospel, Mark quotes the Old Testament prophet Isaiah (Isaiah 40:3), referring to John the Baptist:

the voice of one crying out in the wilderness:
"Prepare the way of the Lord,
make his paths straight." (Mark 1:3 NRSV)

Whereas in *The Voice* singers want their own voice to be recognized and affirmed, John as "the voice" points away from himself to the Lord. From his birth John had been marked as special. Like Sarah (Isaac's mother) and Hannah (Samuel's mother), John's mother, Elizabeth, was barren. John's father, Zechariah, was a priest, and he and Elizabeth were now getting on in years. One day, when Zechariah was serving in the temple, an angel appeared to him telling him that Elizabeth would bear a son who would turn many Israelites back to God. The angel told Zechariah that his son "will bring back many of the people of Israel to the Lord their God. And he will go on before the Lord, in the spirit and power of Elijah, to turn the hearts of the parents to their children and the disobedient to the wisdom of the righteous—to make ready a people prepared for the Lord" (Luke 1:16-17). Zechariah was shocked and unnerved; in disbelief he protested that he and Elizabeth were too old. Because of this unbelief, the angel told him that he would be unable to speak until the child was born. Just as with Sarah and Hannah, Elizabeth miraculously became pregnant and gave birth to a son, John. Only once Zechariah confirmed that the boy should be called John was his speech restored.

John (who was born just a few months before his cousin Jesus) grew into a young man, and the word of God came to him as it had to the Old Testament prophets. He went into the area by the Jordan River and began to preach a remarkable message: "God the great King is on his way. Make your paths straight and your roads level." The imagery here is of a truly great king coming with his entourage from far away. Despite the great roads built by the Romans, many roads remained in poor condition. Such is the magnitude of the coming visit by the King that the roads need to be leveled so that he and his entourage can proceed with ease to their destination.

Even today we are familiar with such preparations. In the UK when the Queen visits a town everything is spruced up, and if you know she is coming to your house, you clean and paint and make sure everything is spick and span, ready to receive Her Majesty.

However, *roads* as used by John the Baptist is a metaphor. The roads that need to be leveled and spruced up are the hearts of God's people.

God, as we have seen, is holy and cannot tolerate sin, and so God's people need to turn away from their sins. The word in the Bible for this is *repent*, to clean out the innermost parts of our being so that they are ready when God arrives.

John's preaching caused a great stir, with large crowds going out into the wilderness to listen to him. The Pharisees, Sadducees, and Zealots could not ignore this tumult and excitement, and many of them also went out to hear what John was saying. John was fearless in his call for repentance, including repentance from the leaders. He would address them directly, calling all to repent and to show their repentance by being baptized by him in the River Jordan. On one occasion, for example, when John saw Pharisees and Sadducees approaching where he was baptizing, he rebuked them in very strong language: "You brood of vipers! Who warned you to flee from the coming wrath? Produce fruit in keeping with repentance." He reminded them that mere descent from Abraham was insufficient. Their faith needed to show in their lives (Matthew 3:7-10).

We can only imagine what the Pharisees and Sadducees thought of such preaching. What an affront for this desert preacher to speak to them about repentance and judgment! Who did he think he was? When God acted, as they all hoped he would do, he would judge their enemies, not *them*. John was surely only another of those strange, wild preachers who arose from time to time.

Israel entered the Promised Land by crossing over the River Jordan, as we saw in chapter eleven. John's choice of this place for his preaching is highly significant and symbolic. He is saying, "God is coming, and this will be your great chance to really enter the land, to really return from exile, to really become what God intended you to be."

Doubtless, most of the Pharisees, Sadducees, and Zealots were highly skeptical of John. After all, who was he? He wasn't part of any of their official organizations; he hadn't trained under their instruction; indeed, they had never heard of him before. Nevertheless, John's preaching that God was coming and the attention it was gaining must have focused their thinking and hopes. Remember, they all had their own view of how God would intervene when he chose to do so. The Zealots, for example, must have hoped that at last a great military leader would arise who would lead them in throwing off Roman rule once and for all.

John attracted many followers, some of whom attached themselves to him permanently to be instructed by him and to learn everything they could from him. Such followers of a teacher were called *disciples*. But John makes it absolutely clear that he is not "the One." Rather the One is on his way, and John is only "the voice" preparing for the coming of the One. The One is more powerful than John. Even as a prophet John states he is not worthy even to untie the One's sandals or to carry them, as a slave might do. John explains to the people that although he baptizes people in water, when the One arrives, he will baptize people in the Holy Spirit. Who is this person John was speaking of? It surely could not be the anticipated Messiah, could it? He was to be a warrior king who would remove the Israelites from Roman bondage. So who was he, and how could he immerse people in the very Spirit of God? This was a remarkable but perplexing message. What could it mean?

READINGS: Luke 1:5-24 and 57-80

THE ONE

THE COMING OF "THE ONE" about whom John the Baptist spoke was quite different from what most first-century Jews expected or hoped for. The Old Testament prophets had pointed to a *Messiah* (meaning "anointed one" or "anointed king") as they looked into the future when God would act to fulfill his purposes in his creation and with his people. John the Baptist, when he spoke of the One, was indicating that the Messiah was about to arrive. First-century Jews had their own ideas of what a messiah, a king, should look like when he arrived.

We, too, have our own ideas of what celebrities should be like: they ought to arrive in a limousine, have bodyguards, dress in the most expensive fashion, live in fabulous houses on large properties, secure behind big walls. When they travel it should be in their private jet; they should only stay at the most expensive hotels and be generally inaccessible to ordinary mortals like ourselves.

It is completely different with the One. He was indeed of great lineage; his ancestry could be traced back to Abraham and to King David, so that when Matthew wrote his Gospel he referred to the One as the son of Abraham and the son of David (Matthew 1:1). But the One was born in the humblest circumstances and to the most ordinary of Jewish families. The One's mother was an ordinary peasant Jewish woman named Mary. How could he be the long-awaited Messiah?

The One's conception, nonetheless, already indicated that there was something very special about him. Mary was engaged to be married to her fiancé, Joseph, a carpenter. And then Mary was visited by the angel, Gabriel, with a startling message:

> "You will conceive and give birth to a son, and you are to call him Jesus. He will be great and will be called the Son of the Most High. The Lord God will give him the throne of his father David, and he will reign over Jacob's descendents forever; his kingdom will never end."
>
> "How will this be," Mary asked the angel, "since I am a virgin?"
>
> The angel answered, "The Holy Spirit will come on you, and the power of the Most High will overshadow you. So the holy one to be born will be called the Son of God."
>
> "I am the Lord's servant," Mary answered. "May your word to me be fulfilled." Then the angel left her. (Luke 1:31-35, 38)

Mary's response to this extraordinary news is exemplary: "I am the Lord's servant." It is a response of trust compared with that of Zechariah, John the Baptist's father, who responded with disbelief and doubt when he received a message from an angel.

We can only imagine Joseph's turmoil and sleepless nights when he heard that Mary was pregnant. How had this happened? It would be a terrible scandal, and so he made plans to quietly break off the engagement. But before he could do this, an angel appeared to him and told him not to be afraid to marry Mary, for the child was from the Holy Spirit. And so they wed.

As the angel had told her, Mary's son would be named Jesus, which means "God saves," because he would rescue his people from their sins. We also learn from his virgin conception that though he would be fully human, his father—in some mysterious way—would not be Joseph but God. Jesus is the Son of God. Although born in such humble circumstances, he is also the Son of David about whom the prophets spoke, and he will turn out to be the greatest king the world has ever seen.

Jesus was born away from Mary and Joseph's home, which was in Nazareth, because his parents had to travel to Bethlehem for a census. Mary wrapped him in cloth and laid him in a manger. But even here amazing things happened. An angel—one of God's great messengers—appeared to shepherds in Bethlehem out in the night tending to their flocks. He announced to them the good news that the Messiah had been born. Suddenly he was accompanied by hundreds of angels, praising God and saying,

> Glory to God in the highest heaven,
> and on earth peace to those on whom his favor rests. (Luke 2:14)

They rushed off to find Mary and Joseph and to see the newly born child, Jesus.

King Herod ruled over Judea at this time and rumors reached him of the birth of a king among his people. Such rumors should never be taken lightly by those wanting to hold on to power, so Herod assigned his staff to pursue all avenues to track down this newborn king. When he realized that he had been tricked by some foreign astrologers (whom we know as the "three wise men") who had come to worship this newborn king, he issued a terrible command: all children in and around Bethlehem—where the king was supposed to have been born—who were under two years of age were to be killed. Joseph and Mary fled to Egypt, and only later, when they heard that Herod had died, did they return to Judea, coming up out of Egypt just as Israel had done hundreds of years before (see Matthew 2:15). You will recall that when God rescued the Israelites from Egypt, he brought them to himself. Could it be that through Jesus God is doing something similar but now on a global scale?

As Jesus grew up, his parents would take him to Jerusalem for the regular festivals there. When he was twelve years old, Joseph and Mary were on their way home again when they discovered, to their consternation, that they could not find him. One can imagine their rising panic as they searched for him among their fellow travelers. Returning to Jerusalem, they searched all over for him. After three days and sleepless nights, they found him in the temple sitting among the teachers, listening to them and asking questions.

Those who heard him were amazed at his wisdom. Not surprisingly his parents rebuked him, but astonishingly he replied, "Why were you searching for me? . . . Didn't you know I had to be in my Father's house?" (Luke 2:49). Already at twelve years old, Jesus was conscious of his special relationship with God. The temple was where God lived in the midst of his people, and Jesus evocatively refers to it as "my Father's house."

We know virtually nothing about Jesus between the age of twelve and the age of about thirty. We can only wonder and imagine what these years of his life were like. As Jesus grew and matured into a man, Mary and Joseph must often have wondered what lay in store for him. Doubtless, as they lay in bed at night, now more or less fifty years old, from time to time they reminisced about his special birth, the messages they received from the angel's visits, their flight to Egypt and then their return, that time when they couldn't find him on the way back from Jerusalem, and just what a wonderful son he was. But, for years now, things had been quiet and family life had assumed a normal rhythm. Their other children were doing well, and Jesus had become a fine carpenter under the tutelage of his father, Joseph. Doubtless, they were proud at his success in this area. Wouldn't it be wonderful if life carried on peacefully as it was?

READING: Luke 2

JESUS BEGINS HIS
PUBLIC LIFE

KING DAVID SHOT FROM obscurity to fame after he defeated Goliath, as we saw in chapter fourteen. Similarly, Jesus' early life was spent in relative obscurity. His birth caused a stir, to be sure. And when, in his early years, Mary and Joseph would travel up to Jerusalem to go to the temple, invariably strange things happened, with individuals recognizing that Jesus was the promised one, the Messiah (Luke 2:22-40).

But apart from Jesus' immediate circle, most of that was forgotten as the years passed. What was capturing people's attention around the time Jesus turned thirty was this fiery preacher, John the Baptist, calling the Jews to repentance and speaking of the one who was shortly to arrive on the scene. In many ways John's preaching was the signal for Jesus to emerge from obscurity.

One day Jesus went out to where John was preaching and baptizing in the desert and presented himself to be baptized. John was constantly speaking about "the One" who was coming, but he must have been shocked when it suddenly dawned on him that his cousin, whom he'd grown up with, was really the One. Nothing like this had ever happened to John before, and he tried to prevent Jesus from being baptized, saying "I need to be baptized by you, and do you come to me?" (Matthew 3:14). John instinctively recognized that he was a sinner who needed to be rescued by Jesus from his sins. Jesus reassured John that God had ordained John to baptize him, so John consented. As Jesus emerged from the waters of baptism, something extraordinary happened: the skies broke open and God's Spirit descended on Jesus like a dove. God's voice from heaven spoke, saying, "This is my Son, whom I love; with him I

am well pleased" (Matthew 3:17).

We can learn so much from Jesus' baptism. First, we encounter here a profound insight into what God is like, which is emphasized throughout the New Testament. God the Father speaks from heaven, God the Spirit descends on Jesus in the form of a dove, and God the Son ("This is my Son") is Jesus. And yet we know very clearly from the story thus far that God is one and not three. This is the great mystery of what Christians call the doctrine of the Trinity, that God is one but also three persons, so that relationality is built into the very nature of God.

Second, we receive key insights into Jesus' mission. Jesus, as the Son of God, should be baptizing John. Instead, by insisting he go down into the waters of baptism, Jesus identifies himself in the most profound way with sinners who need to be cleansed of their sin, forgiven by God. If this is the promised Messiah, the king, then he is not at all the sort of king people were expecting. He has not come to lord it over us like many a king would do, but he has come as a servant to seek and save the lost and is willing to pay whatever price is necessary to achieve his mission. When the Father says from heaven, "This is my Son, whom I love; with him I am well pleased," it confirms that this is indeed the mission Jesus is to pursue.

Jesus' life echoes Israel's history in remarkable ways. Just as Israel wandered in the wilderness for forty years, after his baptism Jesus was led by the Spirit into the desert for forty days. While Israel faltered in the wilderness, complaining of a lack of food and doubting God, Jesus fasted, remaining steadfast to God throughout. When at last Jesus became weak and famished, God's enemy, the devil, came to him with three massive temptations. First, the devil taunted him saying, "If you are the Son of God, tell these stones to become bread." Second, he took Jesus to the top of the temple and taunted him again: if you are the Son of God, throw yourself off and the angels will catch you. Third, he showed him the kingdoms of the world and offered all to him if he would only worship the devil. Likewise Israel was tempted to worship other gods in the wilderness and, in contrast to Jesus, they gave in to this by infamously making the golden calf.

What are we to make of these temptations? Recall what the Father said at Jesus' baptism: "This is my Son." Jesus' mission to save sinners is the very last thing the devil wants. He deviously tempts Jesus to adopt a different mission, to use his miraculous powers to avoid the pain and suffering that his mission already involves and will involve. The devil distorts quotes from the Old Testament, lying in his attempt to get Jesus to abandon the servant route shown at his baptism. Surely Jesus will seize the power available to him to make his life easier and gain power over the world. But Jesus steadfastly resists the temptations by quoting the Bible back to the devil. At last the devil leaves him, and we read that "angels came and attended him."

Jesus emerges from the period in the wilderness with his mission focused and clear. He takes on the mission given to Abraham and Israel hundreds of years before—to be a blessing to all nations, a mission Israel had so far failed to accomplish. He has come to rescue sinners, to bring them back to God. How, we wonder, will he go about doing this?

We then see yet another parallel to Israel in the Old Testament—Jesus selects twelve individuals to follow him in his ministry. Jacob had twelve sons who became fathers of twelve tribes (chapter seven). Similarly, Jesus calls twelve men to become his disciples; Jesus is reconstituting the very people of God. In Mark's Gospel we read that Jesus

> appointed twelve that they might be with him and that he might send them out to preach and to have authority to drive out demons. These are the twelve he appointed: Simon (to whom he gave the name Peter), James son of Zebedee and his brother John (to them he gave the name Boanerges, which means "sons of thunder"), Andrew, Philip, Bartholomew, Matthew, Thomas,

James son of Alphaeus, Thaddaeus, Simon the Zealot and Judas Iscariot, who betrayed him. (Mark 3:13-19)

Here we get an insight into what it meant to be one of Jesus' disciples. First of all, the disciples were called to be *with Jesus*. They left their jobs and lived with him 24-7 as he went about his public life. Jesus invested deeply in this group, shaping and forming them for their future role in what he was initiating, and we can tell from the nicknames he gave them that he knew them well. Simon was given the name *Peter* by Jesus, which means "rock"; Jesus recognized in Peter a future leader in what he was starting. James and John are called "sons of thunder," perhaps because they had such short fuses. We might wonder what kind of people Jesus called to be this inner group of his most intimate followers. They were ordinary but often surprising. Several were fishermen. Matthew had been a despised tax collector, working for the occupying power of Rome. We cannot be sure, but it is possible that Simon the Zealot had been part of the Zealots, the Jewish group that thought Roman rule over Judea should be removed by force. And with Judas we get an inkling of trouble that lies ahead: this is the one who will betray Jesus. This was an imperfect group, but as we have seen and will continue to see, God uses imperfect people to accomplish his will in the world.

Second, the disciples were called to share in Jesus' public activity. As we will see, Jesus preached and taught as he moved around the country, and the Twelve were called to help with that work. We will also see that Jesus regularly performed miracles, and once again the disciples were called to participate; in the quote above, exorcising demons was one particular work they were called to do.

The foundations are now laid for Jesus' public work. His baptism and the temptations in the wilderness provide laser-sharp focus for his mission. He is here to save sinners. It will not be an easy path but one of endurance and suffering that will test every fiber of his being. The team now assembled around him will learn all they can as they observe him in action day in and day out, helping with his public activities. But just what form will this difficult mission take? We will soon see.

READINGS: Matthew 3:13–4:11 and 4:18-22

23

WHAT JESUS TAUGHT

I N THE UNITED KINGDOM there is still a monarchy, while the USA is a republic. Many Americans are still just as fascinated by the royal family as most British citizens. We all know, however, that the Queen's authority is extremely limited. The royal family may be of great symbolic value in the United Kingdom and the Commonwealth, but we would all be shocked if the Queen expected her words and thoughts to be taken as law.

Jesus, however, came into a world that understood the near absolute power of kingship. One reason the Jews found Roman rule so distressing was that Caesar's authority in his empire was absolute. There was no area of life, be it family, business, leisure, sports, trade, religion, or anything else, in which Caesar's rule was not total. To grasp the radical nature of Jesus' message, we need to imagine ourselves back in such a world, a world in which kings were indeed kings and in which they did not tolerate rivals. It may seem strange that Jesus could become a rival with his humble approach, but indeed he did. What could he have said or done to cause this?

In his three years of public life, approximately from the age of thirty to thirty-three, Jesus taught and did an enormous amount. In fact the Gospel writer John (not the same John as John the Baptist) concluded his account of Jesus' life by saying, "Jesus did many other things as well. If every one of them were written down, I suppose that even the whole world would not have room for the books that would be written" (John 21:25). Jesus' three years of teaching and doing were packed. And so we need to ask, if we traveled around listening to him preach and teach, as did the disciples, what would be the core theme of his message?

Fortunately, the Gospels summarize the heart of Jesus' message from time to time. Mark 1:14-15 is one such summary passage: "After John was put in prison, Jesus went into Galilee, proclaiming the good news of God. 'The time has come,' he said. 'The kingdom of God has come near. Repent and believe the good news!'"

"Good news!" What comes to mind when you hear these words? If you are a mother of energetic kids, you may think, *School will soon be starting again; that is really good news.* Or perhaps you will soon be going on vacation, or you just got the job of your dreams. Or maybe you have recently met the person who you think will be your soulmate for life. All of these things are good news, but the Greek word Jesus uses is a much stronger one than this. The word has its background in the prophecies of the Old Testament and refers to that time when God will act to deal with sin, to establish his people, and to restore his good creation. This is unique, epochal news on a truly cosmic scale. John the

Baptist preached that God was on his way. The good news Jesus tells is that God has arrived in Jesus and that he is at work turning history around so that it will never be the same again. God is breaking into history and turning things around so that the creation can be led toward the destiny he always intended for it.

The kingdom of God has come near; it has arrived. The kingdom of God is simply a way of speaking about the reign of God. God, as we have seen, created the world and so rightly is its King. But as children of Adam and Eve, we are rebels against our rightful King. Now with the coming of Jesus, the reign of God has broken in; the turning point of history has been reached. God is intervening to recover his purposes for his creation and for us his creatures.

As we have seen, this was the message that all the major groups in Judaism were longing to hear. But when they looked at Jesus' humble birth and low profile, they found his message confusing—and so do we. If God's kingdom had really come, why were the Romans not being beaten up and overthrown? Where was the superhuman military might to destroy the enemies of the Jews and to re-establish the glory days of Israel?

This is where it is vital to get Jesus' message right. All the Jewish groups were looking for *one* intervention by God to establish his reign and route his enemies. Jesus divides that one intervention into *two phases* with a very important time in between.

Jesus teaches that if he is present as the Son of God, then God's kingdom has indeed come; it has arrived. As we can see from Jesus' birth, his low-profile growth to adulthood, and his public life, however, Jesus does not come with the armies of heaven that he rightly commands. He is born to a peasant mother, he grows up to be a humble carpenter, and even when he begins his public life, he does so as a relative unknown. He comes as a servant to live and die so that God's kingdom can be opened to all who are willing to repent and believe in Jesus. As the Son of God, Jesus wields far more power than any emperor or Pharaoh who has ever lived. But at his first coming he sets that power and glory aside to live and die to bring us and his world back to God.

However, Jesus teaches that he will come again a second time, and when he comes again, he will come on the clouds of heaven with all the authority that rightly belongs to him as the Son of God. At this second coming he will come as a mighty judge to roll up the carpet of history and usher in the new heavens and the new earth.

Thus on the one hand, Jesus teaches that with his coming the kingdom of God has arrived, and yet when he teaches his disciples, he instructs them to pray, "your kingdom come, your will be done" (Matthew 6:10), a prayer that looks forward to the final and full reign of God at Jesus' second coming.

Why these two phases? Jesus' name means "God saves." According to the Bible, his first coming is designed to set in motion the salvation of those anywhere in the world who will submit to him as their King. He came first as one of us, incognito, with his glory hidden to create space for humans to respond to him or reject him.

How does Jesus hope that his hearers will respond to him? As Mark says, "Repent and believe the good news." Or, as the Good News Bible translates this verse, "Turn away from your sins and believe the Good News!" (Mark 1:15 NIV, GNT). To repent is to change your mind about yourself, to go from seeing yourself as fine and basically good to seeing yourself as a rebel against God and as someone who needs God's forgiveness. To believe the good news is to accept Jesus' offer of amnesty, of forgiveness of sins, so that you can be reconciled to the God for whom you were made.

The four Gospels contain a great deal of what Jesus taught. As he travels from place to place, he teaches in the Jewish synagogues and to crowds out in the open as well as interacting one on one. Jesus is a gifted teacher. The longest recorded sermon of Jesus, and the most well-known, is the so-called Sermon on the Mount (Matthew 5–7). Not surprisingly its main theme is the kingdom of God or heaven. Jesus teaches about the characteristics of the citizens of his kingdom (Matthew 5:3-12), the influence on the world they will have if they really live like this (Matthew 5:13-16), how they are to think about the laws of the Old Testament, how to pray (the Lord's Prayer [Matthew 6:5-14]), and so on. He concludes by telling his hearers that if they live like this, they will build the house of their lives on solid rock rather than on shifting sand (Matthew 7:24-27).

Often Jesus taught in a story form, in what are called *parables*, and hearers would be left wondering just what he was getting at. This was his intention, to stir his audience to think hard about what was going on in their midst and come to their own decision about who he was and how they should respond. An example is Jesus' parable of the farmer who went out to sow

seed (Matthew 13:1-23), an image that Jesus' audience would immediately identify with. Some seed fell on the path and was snatched up by the birds. Some fell on rocky places and sprang up but soon withered from the sun. Some fell among thorns and grew up only to be choked by the thorns. Some, however, fell on good soil and produced an enormous crop! The seed stands for Jesus' teaching, and the hearers are challenged on what kind of soil they are as they are invited to receive Jesus' teaching and let it do great things in and through them.

Jesus' message was truly good news. One day he and his disciples went up a mountain. His core group of disciples—James, John, and Peter—stayed with him to pray. Suddenly they were amazed. Jesus was transformed before them so that they got a sense of his true greatness and power and authority. Moses, representing the Law—the first five books of the Bible—and Elijah, representing the prophets, appeared and talked with Jesus about his forthcoming "exodus." Typically, Peter felt he had to speak and offered what seemed to him like a good plan—namely, to build a hut each for Jesus, Moses, and Elijah so they could all stay on the mountain. Peter failed to understand that Jesus needed to go down the mountain and finish the work he had come to do—namely, to lead the whole of creation (and not just those enslaved by Egypt) in an exodus from sin and God's judgment.

Jesus' message certainly includes each one of us, inviting us to return home to the God who made us for himself. But it is also far bigger than that. Jesus' message and the mission he is busy with aims at healing the creation as far as the curse is found. This is truly good news!

READINGS: Mark 1:14-45 and Matthew 13:18-23

24

WHAT JESUS DID

WE HAVE ALL MET people who say one thing but do another. In fact, this is true of us all to some extent. But the bigger the gap is between what people say and what they do, the more frustrating it can be.

If you travel to London, you will find yourself using the underground train system (affectionately known as the Tube), and sooner or later you will hear the announcement, "Mind the gap!" At some stations there is a slight gap between the train door you exit from and the platform, and the announcement is to remind you to pay attention so that you don't trip over the uneven space in between.

Astonishingly, with Jesus, there is no gap. We have seen what remarkable things he had to say, preaching all over the place, instructing his band of disciples, telling stories that still make us stop and think, all part of his overarching message that with him the kingdom of God had arrived!

But Jesus didn't just speak about the reign of God. He also demonstrated it in his miracles and embodied it in his lifestyle. The kingdom of God is all about God rescuing his creation—that includes us—from sin and its devastating effects, bringing wholeness and healing. Not surprisingly, therefore, one thing that Jesus did throughout his public years was to heal people, bringing the wholeness of the kingdom where there was only brokenness and pain. We offer four examples out of many possibilities.

First, in Jesus' time leprosy was a terrible disease. It meant that you were regarded as unclean and excluded from all the joys of normal family and social life. Can you imagine? Always excluded: never touched, never held, never hugged. A living agony of exclusion, even as the leprosy ate away at your flesh. This disabling disease made it harder and harder to survive by yourself even while it increased your rejection by society.

One day such a man, a leper, came in desperation to Jesus, kneeling before him and begging Jesus to make him clean. Jesus was moved with compassion. He understood and sympathized with the plight of this man. He reached out and touched the man, saying "I am willing; be clean." Immediately the man was cleansed from his leprosy (see Mark 1:41). This was one of the many remarkable miracles Jesus performed, as you will find by reading any of the four Gospels in the New Testament.

This miracle shows us Jesus' power to heal as only God can—but that's not all. It also shows Jesus' knowledge of the heart. He understands the man needs his body to be fixed, but he knows that the man's pain and brokenness run much deeper. Before healing the leper, Jesus does what no one else would do, he reaches out and touches him, a profound gesture through which Jesus affirms his humanity. It is no wonder that even though Jesus tells him to go and tell no one, the healed man goes out telling everyone what Jesus has done for him! Thus the healing of this leper provides a clear picture of God's kingdom—bringing healing and wholeness by erasing the effect of sin and rebellion in God's world. We now see more clearly why Jesus brought truly "good news." This miracle was another way of announcing that the kingdom was at hand, the kingdom foretold in the Old Testament (see Isaiah 29:18-21; 61:1-3; 65:17-19).

A second miracle of note involves demons. Although there is much we do not understand about the demonic, the Bible is clear that demons are real and that, like their father the devil, they specialize in warping life against God's design for it. Jesus encountered a man who was named Legion because he was possessed by many demons (Mark 5:1-5). He was incredibly strong and could not be restrained. His life was a constant nightmare. He lived alone in the cemetery among the dead where he could be heard restlessly howling away and trying to harm himself with stones. Jesus encountered him and fearlessly commanded the unclean spirits to exit the man. When the demons requested they be cast into a herd of pigs, Jesus agreed. Jews were not supposed to eat pork as it was forbidden in the Old Testament and regarded as "unclean." The demons thus thought they could find a temporary refuge in the pigs, who were unlikely to be eaten any day soon. But as they entered the pigs, the pigs rushed over a cliff and drowned in the lake. The pigs were innocent but here become caught up in the collateral damage of evil. Unsurprisingly the pig herders ran off and told the story. When people came to investigate, they could hardly believe their eyes: there was the previously possessed man sitting with Jesus, clothed and in his right mind! Again we witness the power of Jesus over evil—but we also see what the kingdom of God is all about. It is God cleansing his good creation from evil and its terrible effects, taking the forces of evil head-on and defeating them.

Jesus is King over both disease and the demonic. In another miracle, he shows that he is also King over nature. The Jews were not a seafaring nation, and it's unlikely that Jesus' disciples could swim. But even if they could, what happened to them one evening was downright scary (Mark 4:35-41). Jesus had asked his disciples to go to the other side of the lake with him, so they all piled into a boat. As they were crossing, a terrific storm blew up on the Sea of Galilee, as it does from time to time, and the boat was in danger of capsizing.

Where was Jesus? Asleep in the boat in the middle of this terrible storm! The disciples shook him awake and then watched in awe as he stood up and rebuked the wind, commanding the sea, "Quiet! Be still!" Immediately the winds died down and it was completely calm. The disciples "were terrified and asked each other, 'Who is this? Even the wind and the waves obey him!'" (Mark 4:41). In the Old

Testament (see Psalm 107:29) it is only God who calms the storm. Through this miracle Jesus shows himself to be God.

Finally, one of the most important miracles Jesus performed demonstrated his power over death itself. According to Genesis 3, death is a result of the rebellion of the first couple, Adam and Eve, and of our rebellion against God. This fourth miracle involves Jesus' close friends—the siblings Lazarus, Mary, and Martha. Lazarus died, and by the time Jesus arrived at his house, he had already been in his tomb for four days. Jesus was taken to the grave, and after praying, he shouted, "Lazarus, come out." And then: "The dead man came out, his hands and feet wrapped with strips of linen, and a cloth around his face. Jesus said to them, 'Take off the grave clothes and let him go'" (John 11:44). Jesus even has power over death.

These four miracles show Jesus' power over disease, demons, nature, and death. As you can imagine, Jesus' miracles attracted huge crowds and people were asking, "Who is this man?" At a key point in his public ministry Jesus asked his disciples, "But what about you? . . . Who do you say I am?" Peter answered, "You are the Messiah" (Mark 8:29). This answer from Peter showed that he understood Jesus was the promised King about whom the Old Testament prophets spoke. He had now come to usher in God's reign and to save the world from sin. Remarkably, Jesus sternly ordered Peter to tell no one about this. Why?

As mentioned in chapter nineteen, all the major Jewish groups were looking for the Messiah. Jesus' miracles revealed his power, and one danger was that one of these groups would try to co-opt Jesus to fulfill its agenda. But the greater danger was that Jesus' incredible claims—to be the Messiah and the Son of God—would become too controversial too quickly, triggering a major confrontation with the religious and political leaders prematurely. For, be in no doubt, major confrontation was brewing. The sort of claims Jesus was making and enacting were starting to call forth opposition from the religious and political leaders, as the absolute authority Jesus claimed began to dawn on them. As his message started to sink in, Jesus' claim that God's reign had broken in with his arrival on the scene upset both the Jews and the Romans.

READINGS: Mark 1:40-45; 4:35-41; 5:1-17; John 11

25

FATAL CONFRONTATION

J ESUS' PUBLIC LIFE generated mixed responses. Many loved him, and his followers were often the most unexpected people: prostitutes, despised tax collectors, people healed from debilitating illnesses and demon possession, fishermen, and so forth. But as Jesus gained popularity, the religious establishment (based especially in Jerusalem) and the political establishment (centered in Rome but well represented in Judea) became more and more aware of the threat Jesus presented.

As we've seen, the major Jewish groups had their own views of what things should look like when God intervened decisively in history, and Jesus did not line up with their expectations. As gentle as Jesus could be, he was also not averse to calling out religious leaders for their hypocrisy. In this respect he was much like John the Baptist. The movement generated around him inevitably threatened the leaders' own power bases, and what's more, many of the things he said sounded downright heretical.

The Jews were well versed in the Old Testament, and when, for example, Jesus went around saying things to people like, "Your sins are forgiven," his opponents rightly understood that he was claiming God's authority, and they were quick to cry out, "Blasphemy!" He did just this in an extraordinary event while at home in Capernaum. A huge crowd gathered so that it was impossible to get near him. Some men came carrying a paralyzed man on a mattress, and when they could not get through the crowd to Jesus, they came up with an ingenious plan. It was not hard in houses of those days to make a hole in the roof, which they did, and then they lowered the man down on his mat. Jesus was impressed with their faith and said to the paralyzed man, "Your sins are forgiven" (Mark 2:5). Some of the authorities present immediately thought, "Claiming to forgive sins like God is blasphemy!" In order to show them that he did indeed have God's authority, he then healed the man.

In America, where freedom of speech is guaranteed, blasphemy may not sound serious. "What's the problem?" But according to the Old Testament, taking God's name in vain merits the death penalty. This enables us to see that the sort of opposition Jesus evoked was serious and potentially very dangerous. But the religious leaders' concern had an added political and practical dimension. They worried that Jesus and his followers would incite rebellion against Rome, resulting in Rome crushing the nation even further than it already had (Luke 23:14; John 11:49-50). They did not want the nation to suffer unnecessarily.

If Jesus made the religious leaders nervous, he did the same with the political leaders. The Jews saw God as King over everything, and implicit in Jesus' claim to be God is a claim to rule over everything, including Caesar and the Roman Empire. Rome was extremely wary of challenges to its power, knowing well how easily such confrontations could spiral out of control, and so they stamped out such efforts as early as possible, and did so brutally. One of their very worst forms of punishment was crucifixion, nailing a criminal to a cross, which resulted in a slow and extraordinarily painful death.

No one, including Jesus' disciples, thought that the promised Messiah—the King!—would be crucified. Such a possibility was not even vaguely on anyone's radar screen. And yet, toward the end of his three years of public life Jesus deliberately puts himself in a position for the final, fatal confrontation to take place. We said in chapter twenty-one that as a teenager Jesus referred to the temple as his Father's house. The temple was in Jerusalem, the center and heartbeat of Jewish life. Jews were required by their law to visit it several times each year and the biggest festival was that of the Passover, when they would remember that their ancestors were enslaved in Egypt and were rescued by God and brought out of Egypt to himself.

At this point in the Bible's story, critical events happen rapidly. Jesus knows that the opposition against him is escalating, and yet he still decides to go to Jerusalem to celebrate the Passover. He make a triumphal entry into Jerusalem riding on a donkey, with the crowds acclaiming him as the Messiah. Whereas before he had often encouraged people, like Peter, not to speak about him as the Messiah, now he comes out openly as such. If that wasn't enough, he goes to his Father's house, the temple, and drives out the many corrupt traders in righteous anger, claiming they have turned his Father's house from a house of prayer into den of robbers. One can only imagine how that went down even as thousands of Jews were gathering in Jerusalem for the Passover.

These events are the proverbial straw that breaks the camel's back for his opponents. Religious leaders conspire with political leaders to put a stop once and for all to this madness: Jesus needs to be taken out; it is that simple.

Jesus celebrates the Passover meal with his disciples, but it is unlike any Passover they have ever experienced. As noted in chapter eight, in the final plague before the Israelites left Egypt, blood from slaughtered lambs was put on the doorposts of the houses of the Israelites so that when the firstborns of Egypt were slain, the Israelites were spared. Jesus picks up one of the cups used during the Passover meal and says, "This is my blood of the new covenant." He breaks the unleavened bread and says, "This is my body, which is broken for you" (see Luke 22:19-20). In this way he relates the image of the Passover lamb to himself, claiming that through what was about to happen, he would lead the world in an exodus out of slavery and into freedom and life.

Jesus had told his disciples again and again that his path was ultimately one of terrible suffering, but they found it hard to grasp. And now here he is using the imagery of the Passover to portray himself as the lamb that must be slain. What could this possibly mean? They were soon to find out.

For the religious authorities to find Jesus and arrest him, they need help. Jerusalem is teeming with people. Agonizingly Judas, one of Jesus' twelve disciples, betrays Jesus to them for a price. They find and arrest Jesus and then hand him over to the political leaders who alone can pronounce the death penalty. The political leaders—Pilate and Herod— can find no reason for sentencing Jesus to death and do their best to pass the ball on this one. Ever the pragmatist, Pilate offers another man,

Barabbas, indicted for murder, to be punished instead. The frenzied crowds, incited by the religious leaders, will have none of it. They demand the death of Jesus.

And so Jesus is tortured, mocked, and crucified as the lowest kind of criminal. Once he finally dies after agonizing hours on his cross—with

a soldier piercing his side, causing a flow of water and blood to show that he was truly dead (John 19:34)—a Jewish leader named Nicodemus, who had disagreed with his colleagues in their opposition to Jesus, gets permission to take down his body and bury it in a tomb.

Jesus' disciples flee. All their hopes seem to have been dashed. Jesus had been so extraordinary. They had trusted him. They had be-

lieved him when he said the kingdom had arrived—but where is the kingdom now? Broken on a cross and decaying in a tomb.

Imagine the horror, terror, and despair the disciples must have felt. But as they think back on Jesus' life they might remember what John the Baptist once said about him, "Look, the Lamb of God, who takes away the sin of the world!" (John 1:29). We too easily romanticize such sayings, as we do with the cross. In Jesus' day the cross was the most horrific symbol and form of death. But the key insight is that for the lamb to take away the sins of the world, it must first be slain. And it was on the cross that Jesus was slain, bearing there what humanity deserved. His death was to be the final sacrifice that would rescue the world from sin, death, and judgment.

But for now the disciples do not understand this. They only know the one they had placed their hope and trust in is dead. They are confused and in despair. What are they to do now?

READINGS: John 1:29-34 and Luke 23

ON THE THIRD DAY

WHEN CRAIG WAS a student in Oxford, one of his favorite places was Blackwell Bookstore. From the small exterior and shopfront you might easily miss it, but once you go in it gets bigger and bigger with layer after layer and level after level of all sorts of books.

Jesus and the kingdom of God are like that. Our darkness and brokenness are far worse than anyone cares to admit (see chapter four), but the rescue Jesus brings through his death on the cross is far, far bigger than we can imagine. From the outside, God's kingdom may be easy to miss, but once we get inside we find layers and levels we never could have imagined.

When it comes to the great boundary issues of life like birth and death, women are often far more tuned in than men. It is not altogether surprising then—but nevertheless quite wonderful—that on the third day after Jesus' death, women went first to his tomb. Mary Magdalene came to Jesus' tomb early in the morning while it was still dark. To her shock, the stone door had been rolled away. She hurtled off to Peter and John to tell them that someone had taken Jesus' body away and she had no idea where it now was. Peter and John sprinted off to the tomb, went inside, and saw the linen wrappings that had been around Jesus' body lying where the body had been. What on earth was going on (John 20:1-10)?

Mary needed time alone, and when Peter and John went home, she remained weeping outside the tomb, inconsolable. Like Peter, curiosity got the better of her, and she peered into the tomb, only to see two angels sitting where Jesus' body had been lying. They asked her why she was crying, and she replied, just as she had said to Peter and John, "They have taken my Lord away and I don't know where they have put him."

As she says this, she turned around to see a man standing beside her. He also asked her why she was crying and whom she was looking for. Thinking he was the gardener, she begged him, "Sir, if you have carried him away, tell me where you have put him, and I will get him." The man turned and said one word to her that would change her life—and the world— forever: "Mary." As he said her name, Mary recognized that it was Jesus, risen from the dead. Shocked into recognition, Mary fell at his feet and cried out, "Teacher." Mary left and announced to the disciples, "I have seen the Lord" (John 20:11-18).

In the days that followed, Jesus appeared to many of his followers, showing them that he was truly alive. Most believed, but Thomas, one of the twelve disciples, was not with the others when Jesus appeared to them and he refused to believe, earning himself the nickname "doubting Thomas." He said to them, "Unless I see the nail marks in his hands and put my finger where the nails were, and put my hand into his side, I will not believe" (John 20:25). The wound in the side was from where the spear had been thrust to make sure Jesus was dead.

A week later—it must have been a long week for Thomas—Jesus appeared to Thomas when his disciples were with him. Jesus knew all about Thomas's doubt and said to him, "Put your fingers here on my hands—where the nails were driven through—and put your hand in my side—through which the spear was thrust." Thomas exclaimed, "My Lord and my God!" (John 20:28).

Also during this time after Jesus' resurrection, two disciples are walking to a village called Emmaus, near Jerusalem. A stranger joins them and asks what they are talking about. They reply with surprise at his ignorance and proceed to explain the roller coaster of events around Jesus that had recently taken place. The stranger explains from the Old Testament how all that has happened fits with God's Word and plan. As they approach Emmaus, the stranger makes as if to go on by himself but, since it is evening, they invite him to stay the night with them. They sit down to a meal with him and as he takes bread, blesses it, and breaks it—remember the Last

Supper?—their eyes are opened to recognize Jesus (Luke 24:30-31). Immediately Jesus disappears.

That anyone should die and then rise again three days later is extraordinary. But Jesus' resurrection is far more than a major miracle. Do you see what happened upon Jesus taking, blessing, and breaking the bread? "Their eyes were opened." Where in the story have we heard that expression before? When the first couple, Adam and Eve, rebelled against God by eating of the tree of the knowledge of good and evil, we read that "then the eyes of both of them were opened" (Genesis 3:7), and they knew sin and shame. This link alerts us to the fact that through his cross and resurrection Jesus was reversing the effect of God's judgment upon the world, overcoming death, and blazing the trail into the renewal of the whole creation.

Although it is late, in their excitement the two disciples hasten back to Jerusalem to share this extraordinary news with the other disciples, saying, "It is true! The Lord has risen." While they are excitedly telling them all that had happened, Jesus appears in their midst. They think they are seeing a ghost, but Jesus tells them, "Touch me and see that I am human, flesh and bone." He also asks for something to eat in order to demonstrate to them that he is truly human. They give him broiled fish and he eats.

Jesus remains on earth for forty days after his resurrection. Toward the end of this time Jesus gathers his followers and commissions them to spread the news about him throughout the world and to teach all the nations how to follow Jesus (Matthew 28:16-20). This is known as Jesus' Great Commission. Jesus says he is leaving them now, but he will send the Holy Spirit, who will empower them for this great task he is entrusting to them.

Sometime later, Jesus leads his followers out to Bethany, about two miles from Jerusalem. Bethany was the home of Mary, Martha, and their brother, Lazarus, whom Jesus raised from the dead. Jesus blesses his disciples, and while he is doing so, he ascends into the sky until a cloud blocks him from their sight. This is a literal and visual picture of Jesus returning to God, from whom he had come, now to occupy the position as King over heaven and earth. The disciples return to Jerusalem where they stay together, devoting themselves to prayer, as they absorb all that had taken place. It was mind-blowing how much had happened in a relatively short period of time. They had so come to trust and love Jesus during their three years with him, and then within days that hope was crushed, obliterated when he was crucified. Doubtless they felt mortified as they reflected on how they had abandoned Jesus at his worst time for fear of the power of Rome. And then, even as they fled and hid, overwhelmed with fear and depression, on the third day that unbelievable news came from the women: his tomb is empty. And then to have—each in their own way—encountered him again and again until their hearts could burst with sheer joy that he had risen, and then ascended.

But what exactly would happen now?

This brings us to the end of act four, "The Coming of the King," the central act of the drama of the Bible. The promised Messiah, Jesus, has come. He lived, died, rose, and ascended. Salvation has been accomplished. But now it needs to be extended throughout the world—to all nations.

READINGS: Luke 24 and Acts 1:6-11

THE CHURCH IS BORN

THE LAST FEAST the disciples had attended was the Passover in Jerusalem. And boy, was it a roller coaster. All hell broke loose. Judas—one of the disciples, now dead through suicide—betrayed Jesus, and then the opposition to Jesus escalated out of control, ending in his crucifixion. But then, wondrously, he appeared to the disciples three days later, alive again! Over the following weeks he showed himself several times in a very physical but somehow transformed body to all the disciples. Once he even appeared to several hundred at once. The roller coaster of emotion leveled out, however, when Jesus ascended to heaven, leaving the disciples sure of his resurrection but not quite sure what would come next.

Now we begin act five of our drama of the Bible: "Spreading the News of the King: The Mission of the Church." It is the next feast in Jerusalem, Pentecost, which comes fifty days after the Passover. The disciples and the close followers of Jesus have been keeping a low profile since Jesus' ascension to heaven. They have all gathered in one house for the feast. We can only imagine their thoughts, feelings, fears, and doubts without Jesus. Particularly, they must have been discussing his directive to remain in Jerusalem until the Holy Spirit came to empower them to tell others about Jesus. How would that happen?

Then, suddenly, they hear a sound like a violent wind, a tornado, and it fills the house in which they are sitting. Tongues of fire appear in their midst and one settles on the head of each of them. "All of them were filled with the Holy Spirit and began to speak in other tongues as the Spirit enabled them" (Acts 2:4). These were the tongues of other languages.

The sound of the violent winds immediately attracts a crowd. Jews have come to Jerusalem from all parts of the Roman Empire, as is typical on the occasion of great feasts. When they hear the sounds of their own languages being spoken, they are utterly amazed. The crowd asks,

> "Aren't all these who are speaking Galileans? Then how is it that each of us hears them in our native language? Parthians, Medes and Elamites; residents of Mesopotamia, Judea and Cappadocia, Pontus and Asia, Phrygia and Pamphylia, Egypt and the parts of

> Libya near Cyrene; visitors from Rome (both Jews and converts to Judaism); Cretans and Arabs—we hear them declaring the wonders of God in our own tongues!" . . . They asked one another, "What does this mean?" (Acts 2:7-12)

Others sneer and say disparagingly, "They're drunk!"

Peter gets up and addresses the crowd, preaching an extraordinary sermon. No, he says, we are not drunk! Instead, this is the fulfillment of what the Old Testament promised—namely, that the time would come when God would pour out his Spirit on all people, on young and old, male and female, slave and free (see Joel 2:28-29). And Peter relates this all to Jesus:

> Fellow Israelites, listen to this: Jesus of Nazareth was a man accredited by God to you by miracles, wonders and signs, which God did among you through him, as you yourselves know. This man was handed over to you by God's deliberate plan and foreknowledge; and you, with the help of wicked men, put him to death by nailing him to the cross. But God raised him from the dead, freeing him from the agony of death, because it was impossible for death to keep its hold on him. (Acts 2:22-24)

God, concludes Peter, has made Jesus both Lord and Messiah.

When the crowd hears Peter's sermon, many of them are convinced and deeply shaken. What, they ask, should we do? Peter replies, "Repent and be baptized, every one of you, in the name of Jesus Christ for the forgiveness of your sins. And you will receive the gift of the Holy Spirit. The promise is for you and your children and for all who are far off—for all whom the Lord our God will call" (Acts 2:38-39).

The response is amazing. Some three thousand people welcome Peter's message and are baptized in the name of Jesus. They are indwelt by the Spirit and become the nucleus of the Christian church, the community of followers of Jesus. This is the birthday of the church, the beginning of the new people of God. Those who have become Christians—followers of Jesus—are from all over the Roman world and beyond, and doubtless as they return home they tell about what has happened and how they have come to believe in Jesus. They tell about how they heard the disciples telling the good news in their own language and then how Peter explained to them, using the Old Testament, what was going on. Here we see the Great Commission that Jesus gave to his disciples starting to be fulfilled. These new Christians return to their homes spreading the good news about Jesus throughout Mesopotamia and northern Africa.

However, many of the converts remain in Jerusalem, adopting a remarkable new lifestyle (Acts 2:43-47). The disciples are doing miracles, just as Jesus had done. The Christians share their belongings with one another and make sure that everyone's needs are met. If God has been so good to them, how can they do otherwise? They sell their possessions to ensure no one is in need. Every day they meet together in the temple and give themselves seriously to the teaching of the *apostles*, which means "sent ones," the name for those disciples who formed the twelve who lived with and accompanied Jesus during his public years.

Jesus chose the Twelve to be with him so that they could give eyewitness testimony about him once he had had returned to the Father, and this is precisely what happens. Having come to believe in Jesus, the early Christians cannot get enough of him, and they want to learn all they can about him from the apostles. Their sense of community is tremendous.

They pray and worship and break bread together. "Breaking bread" certainly includes sharing meals, but it probably also includes reenacting the Last Supper among them, a profound ritual through which they recall and embrace all that Jesus had done and is doing for them.

It is hard to hear about the communal life of these early Christians without feeling at a deep level, *Yes! This gets close to what life is all about.* And this is just how we should feel about it. Pentecost was the sign that God was forming a new humanity under his rule. In the judgment of the Tower of Babel (covered in chapter five), God punished humankind by making sure that their different languages would cause confusion and hostility. Just think of the fallout in international relations from that judgment. Pentecost is the reverse of Babel. The diverse languages are there, to be sure, but now they work together in the service of telling the news of Jesus and creating one people of God.

Earlier we noted that whereas the Jews looked for one major intervention by God into history, Jesus' life divided that into two. There is his first coming, and then there is the time when he will come again, as the Bible says, "with great power and glory" (see Mark 13:26). Why this division? Precisely to create the space—the in-between time—for this era of the church, the time of Jesus' followers, empowered by the Spirit, going into all the world to spread the news of Jesus. It is to provide an opportunity for all of the world to be blessed by Jesus, just as God promised Abraham his descendents would be. Just as three thousand were on the day of Pentecost.

This is what act five of the great drama of the Bible is all about—that time of mission when Jesus has asked those who believe in him as the promised Savior to spread the news of him throughout the world.

READINGS: Acts 2 and Genesis 11:1-9

JERUSALEM TO JUDEA
TO THE ENDS OF
THE EARTH

MOST LIKELY YOU HAVE a church (or several!) in your neighborhood. Have you ever wondered how they came to be there? In England, the arrival of Christianity goes back to AD 597, if not earlier, when a monk called Augustine arrived from Rome. Ultimately, if you traced the origins of our churches back step by step, you would eventually come to Pentecost, the great birthday of the church that we looked at in the last chapter.

When you've had a wonderful experience, it's contagious and you can't prevent yourself from telling others. And so it was with the first Christian converts. As they went home to their towns, cities, and countries around the huge Roman Empire they gossiped about the Gospel, the good news about Jesus. As they were led by the Spirit to change their lives and live under the authority of King Jesus, people asked them questions about why they lived the way they did, and again they would tell people the news of Jesus. In this way the church grew and groups of believers sprang up around the Roman Empire and beyond.

In the period between Pentecost and when Christ returns, that time between the coming of Christ and his final return in glory, the great missionary is the Spirit. Humans play a key role, as we have seen with the first converts, but, at best, we accompany the Spirit on his mission. Indeed, long before Pentecost the Spirit had already been at work, preparing for this time.

In chapter nineteen we mentioned the four hundred silent years between the Old Testament and the New Testament, when the voice of prophecy ceased and it seemed God was inactive. But God was not inactive; the stage was quietly being set for Pentecost and beyond.

First, as a result of the Northern Kingdom and then Judah (the Southern Kingdom) going into exile—even many from Judah did not return—there were groups of Jews scattered throughout the Roman Empire who met in synagogues. Here God's Old Testament Word was kept alive. These synagogues provided opportunities for Jesus and his apostles to explain how Jesus fulfilled the Old Testament prophecy they knew well. Second, as we also saw in chapter nineteen, Alexander the Great had intentionally spread Greek culture throughout his empire. An effect of this was that by the time Jesus started his public life, most of the Old Testament had been translated into Greek so that the Old Testament was available in the lingua franca of the day. The Old Testament is three-quarters of the Christian Bible, and for the mission of the church it made a huge difference having this available in Greek.

Third, for all the antagonism Jews understandably felt toward Roman rule, the Pax Romana (the peace of Rome) meant that the mission of the church was born in a huge empire full of good roads and means of travel and communication while largely devoid of military conflicts. All of these factors contributed to the rapid spread of the news of Jesus from Jerusalem, to Judea, to Rome and beyond.

Strangely, another factor also helped spread the news. Just as Jesus' teaching and deeds called forth opposition, the same was true with Jesus' followers. In many ways the apostles and the early Christians continued the ministry of Jesus. The apostles performed miracles, like Jesus, and the early Christians were of one voice in declaring the risen, ascended Jesus to be the Messiah. If the religious and political leaders thought they had stomped on Christianity by crucifying Jesus, they now realized how wrong they were. Hundreds of people were going around doing and saying things just like Jesus!

Frustrated and angry, the religious leaders had the apostles arrested and imprisoned. But during the night an angel came and released them, saying "Go, stand in the temple courts, and tell the people all about this new life" (Acts 5:20). The next day, the local authorities were amazed that the apostles were not securely locked in jail and rearrested them. The apostles appeared before the high priest and his council and were rebuked, flogged, ordered to speak no more about Jesus, and then released. And what did they do? "The apostles left the Sanhedrin, rejoicing because they had been counted worthy of suffering disgrace for the Name. Day after day, in the temple courts and from house to house, they never stopped teaching and proclaiming the good news that Jesus is the Messiah" (Acts 5:41-42). In this way persecution contributed to the spread and growth of the early church.

As you can imagine, the demands on the apostles—the leaders of the emerging, fast-growing church—were immense. Lest those in need be neglected, the church appointed seven deacons to attend to the welfare of the needy among the Christians so that the apostles could devote themselves to the Word of God—the message about Jesus and the Old Testament—and prayer. One of the deacons, Stephen, was clearly multitalented. He preached and performed miracles and was, as a result, hauled before the Jewish council. In his defense Stephen rehearsed the Old Testament story and rebuked his hearers for not embracing Jesus. His audience became enraged, and they dragged Stephen out of the city and stoned him to death, making Stephen the first Christian martyr. A severe persecution of the Christians then broke out, forcing Christians to scatter from Jerusalem into surrounding Judea and Samaria. Ironically, this very persecution served only to spread the news of Jesus farther.

When Stephen was stoned to death, a Pharisee named Saul stood watching with approval, and he took a very active role in the persecution of the Christians that followed Stephen's death. Soon Christianity had its second martyr, James, the brother of the apostle John, put to death at King Herod's command. Saul would later say of those times, "For you have heard of . . . how intensely I persecuted the church of God and tried to destroy it. I was advancing in Judaism beyond many of my own age among my people and was extremely zealous for the traditions of my fathers" (Galatians 1:13-14).

Strengthened by the Spirit, the early Christians were wonderfully courageous in the face of this opposition, but doubtless the name of "Saul" could bring fear to their hearts. Then the most remarkable thing happened. One day Saul was on the road to Damascus, clutching letters from the high priest that gave him permission to bring any of the followers of Jesus he found there back to Jerusalem for trial. Suddenly a blinding light from heaven flashed around Saul.

> He fell to the ground and heard a voice say to him, "Saul, Saul, why do you persecute me?"
>
> "Who are you, Lord?" Saul asked.
>
> "I am Jesus, whom you are persecuting," [the voice] replied. "Now get up and go into the city, and you will be told what you must do."
>
> The men traveling with Saul stood there speechless; they heard the sound but did not see anyone. (Acts 9:4-7)

Saul, now blind, was led into Damascus, where God instructed a Christian named Ananias to go and speak to him. Not surprisingly Ananias was reluctant, but "the Lord said to Ananias, 'Go! This man is my chosen instrument to proclaim my name to the Gentiles and their kings and to the people of Israel'" (Acts 9:15). Obediently, Ananias went to Saul saying, "The Lord—Jesus . . . has sent me so that you may see again and be filled with the Holy Spirit" (Acts 9:17). Immediately Saul regained his sight and was baptized. Saul, the great persecutor of the Christians, became a follower of Jesus. It took a while for the Christians to be convinced he had changed, but Paul—the Greek name equivalent to Saul—went on to become one of the greatest of the early Christian leaders, thinkers, and missionaries, as we will see.

The explosion of the church after the miraculous day of Pentecost, when the Holy Spirit entered the hearts and minds of those present, continued on amid opposition from without *and* from within this new Christian way. We have seen the opposition from without. But sometimes we are our own worst enemies. The apostles were Jewish, and the radical difference between Jews and Gentiles was a huge part of their cultural DNA. The Gentiles were becoming Christians, the name soon given to those who believed in Jesus as the Messiah, but some of the Jewish Christians were wary of this development. The result was a council of early Christian leaders in Jerusalem at which the open door of the church to all, Jew and Gentile, was established once and for all (Acts 15:1-35).

Even before this, Paul had been identified by the church through the Spirit for mission work to the Gentiles. His energy, once directed at persecution of the church, was now redirected toward the mission of the church. He was soon establishing new groups of Christians—churches—in city after city throughout the known world.

READINGS: Acts 7:54–8:1 and 9:1-31

29

PAUL, THE SENT ONE

THE STORY OF THE BIBLE and the good news about Jesus are a lot like an onion—however many layers you peel away, there are more waiting further down. In some ways the basic news about Jesus is very simple, so a child can understand it. But it is also so deep that a lifetime is not enough to explore it fully. If Paul was to lay a solid foundation for his work of planting churches across the Roman Empire, then he needed a time out to think through carefully all that had happened to him and how it all fit together.

After Paul's experience with Jesus on the Damascus Road, he went to Arabia to think and reflect. We cannot be sure, but it is possible that he went to the region of Mount Sinai in Arabia. If so, this is very significant. Earlier we saw that Mount Sinai was where God met with his people after he rescued them from slavery in Egypt (chapter nine). On the mountain he showed himself to them, spoke to them, and established them as his covenant people. There the portable sanctuary was built and filled with God's presence. From there he led them to the Promised Land.

Paul knew the Old Testament backward, but now he needed to re-think it all in the light of Jesus. One can imagine him in the context of Mount Sinai, praying and thinking, starting with Jesus and working backward into the Old Testament and then starting with the Old Testament and moving forward to Jesus. Back and forth he went until he could start to see how it all fit together. Paul emerged as the great thinker of the early church, likely due to this time when he laid a foundation for the rest of his missionary life.

In the early church, as today, every Christian was a missionary. However, the mission of the church was spearheaded by the apostles, and more than anyone else by Paul. Although their leadership was indispensable, they understood that they were not ultimately in charge. Jesus rules over his church by his Spirit, and the apostles moved and traveled at the direction of the Spirit. Indeed, while the church at Antioch was worshiping the Lord and fasting, "the Holy Spirit said, 'Set apart for me Barnabas and Saul for the work to which I have called them'" (Acts 13:2). One of Paul's favorite ways to describe himself was as a servant of Jesus Christ. Jesus is King and at our best we are his servants.

Paul spent the rest of his life traveling and preaching and establishing churches throughout the Roman Empire. The map of his journeys shows just how far and widespread his travels were. As in our own day, the cities were where most people lived. Paul concentrated his attention on the cities of the Roman Empire, clearly realizing that if churches were established there, they could spread the news of Jesus to the surrounding regions. Invariably Paul would start with the Jews in

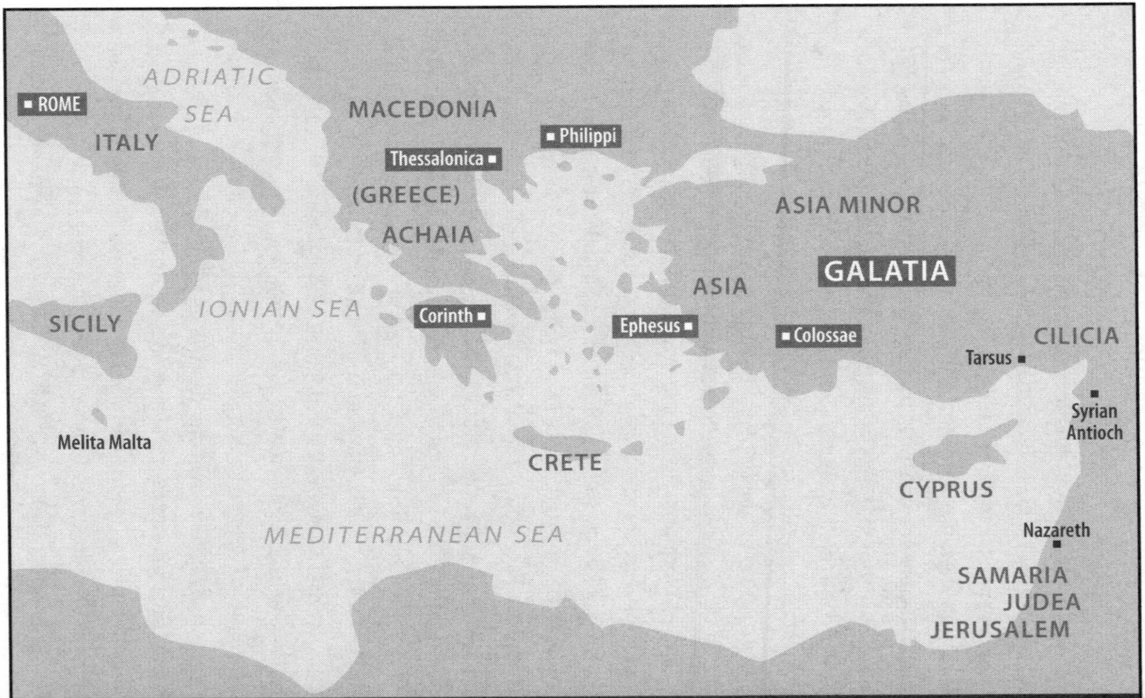

Figure 29.1. Map of Paul's missionary journeys

a new area since they already possessed the Old Testament, and he would make his case for Jesus as the Messiah to them. Then he would expand his ministry to the Gentiles.

Paul would by no means confine himself to preaching to the Jews. For example, when he was in Athens, the famous center of Greek philosophy, he became distressed by all the images of gods in the city. He debated with the Jews in the synagogue and with anyone who would engage with him in the marketplace. Some of the philosophers were irritated by all his talk of Jesus and the resurrection, and so they arranged a formal gathering for him to address them. Paul was wise. Whereas with the Jews he would speak of Jesus in relation to Old Testament prophecy, with Greek philosophers he chose a different approach. Using a statue to an unknown god he had seen in Athens as his basis, he proceeded to tell them about the God of the Bible (Acts 17:16-34).

Like Jesus, Paul suffered regular persecution. Both of us have been to Ephesus, a city that Paul also visited. We saw the great theater, capable of seating thousands of people, that still stands there. In Paul's day a silversmith called Demetrius lived in Ephesus who made his living by crafting shrines. One such shrine was of the goddess Artemis, who in Greek religion was the goddess of wild animals, the hunt, and vegetation, as well as of chastity and childbirth. Demetrius was incensed because Paul's preaching was affecting his business by teaching that gods made with human hands are not gods at all.

Demetrius, an organizer and sort of trade unionist of his day, soon had his fellow silversmiths and the city in uproar. A huge crowd assembled in the theater and for two hours chanted, "Great is Artemis of the Ephesians!" Not surprisingly amid such opposition, Paul left

Ephesus soon after this. Paul suffered a great deal as he traveled the known world speaking of Jesus—he was indicted, charged, imprisoned, persecuted, and run out of town on many occasions. Throughout it all he remained faithful to Jesus' call for him to spread the good news of Jesus throughout the world. As you will see from the map, he was remarkably successful in establishing churches all over the Roman Empire.

Becoming a Christian is a beginning and not an end. It is like being born; once you are alive you need to grow and develop to maturity. The major means the Spirit uses for this are the teachings about Jesus and the fellowship of other Christians. The apostles—apart from Paul—had lived with Jesus and could provide eyewitness testimony about his life and teaching. With the number of new Christians, they were all in great demand. Paul recognized the need to nurture the churches that he had been instrumental in giving birth to. So when he could not visit them, he wrote them letters.

Twelve of his letters are found in the New Testament and they make for fascinating reading. "To all in Rome who are loved by God and called to be his holy people: Grace and peace to you from God our Father and from the Lord Jesus Christ" (Romans 1:7); "to the church of God in Corinth, to those sanctified in Christ Jesus and called to be his holy people, together with all those everywhere who call on the name of our Lord Jesus Christ—their Lord and ours" (1 Corinthians 1:2); and so on. Many New Testament books bear the names of the people Paul wrote to, which correspond to the names of the cities on the map in this chapter. Some letters are short, and a few—such as the letter to the Romans (that is, to the church in Rome)—are very long. All his letters have in common a burning desire to teach his hearers about the way of life in Jesus, encouraging them to keep going and to do justice to the good news in the way they live, remembering all that Jesus has done for them.

With time Paul's twelve letters, letters from other church leaders, and four narratives of the story of Jesus (the Gospels, which encapsulated the eyewitness testimony of the apostles) were collected together to form the New Testament. Together with the Old Testament, this forms what Christians believe to be the written Word of God. The Bible is like the field in which we find hidden that great treasure called Jesus, and this is why to this day when Christians gather, they listen to the Bible read and hear it preached.

The last we hear of Paul is when he is in the capital of the empire, Rome, under house arrest. "For two whole years Paul stayed there in his own rented house and welcomed all who came to see him. He proclaimed the kingdom of God and taught about the Lord Jesus Christ—with all boldness and without hindrance" (Acts 28:30-31). We believe Paul was executed shortly afterward. Peter and many other first-century Christians were also martyred. But the church continued to grow and spread. Mark went to North Africa. Thomas went to India. Within a generation the message of Jesus traveled from Judea and Jerusalem to Rome and beyond.

READINGS: Acts 19 and Philippians 1

30

THE END THAT IS NO END

MANY OF US HAVE READ J. R. R. Tolkien's masterpiece *The Lord of the Rings* or seen the films. Near where I (Craig) live, there is a small village called Ring's End. It always reminds me of *The Lord of the Rings*, of Frodo and his fellow travelers' great adventure, and of how, after destroying the ring, Frodo and his fellow Hobbits return to the Shire. In the final chapter, Frodo is writing his story of all that has taken place. Frodo's closest companion, Sam, comments that Frodo has nearly finished. Frodo replies, "I have quite finished, Sam. . . . The last pages are for you."

As we come to the end of the story of the Bible, this brings us to our day, to our country, city, town, or village. These last pages are for us. From the perspective of the story of the Bible we live in the same age we have been looking at, that of the early Christians—that is, act five, the age of Jesus, the age of the Spirit, the age of mission, the age of the church. This is the age in which we have the freedom to hear the news about Jesus and to make up our minds about him. The story of the Bible is not just another story. It claims to be the true story of the whole world, and it invites us to make it *our* story.

If you read the letters to the churches in the New Testament, you will discover that the churches then were much like churches today. Some were faithful and steady in living for Jesus and telling the news about him. Others were wracked with division and in danger of going off the rails. It remains a good test of a church whether, first, Jesus and the Spirit are central to the life of the church and second, it is faithful, like Paul, in proclaiming the kingdom—the reign of God—and teaching about Jesus from both Old and New Testaments.

As in the New Testament and in the early centuries under Roman rule, Christians continue to live under the reign of Jesus and to tell people about him. And they continue to be persecuted. Indeed, there is hard evidence that Christianity is the most persecuted religion in the world today. One of the images for being a Christian in the New Testament is taking up your cross and following Jesus (Luke 9:23). We know what followed when Jesus took up his cross, and it is the same with many Christians today. Following Jesus is glorious, but it also involves suffering. Jesus' way was that of the cross, so it was with his apostles and the early Christians, and so it is with us today.

The apostle who probably lived the longest was the apostle John. His nickname was Boanerges, which means "son of thunder," perhaps because in his early years he had a short fuse and was prone to violent outbursts. Such people often hide the wounds of their life behind such anger. But by the time we get to the Gospel of John, John is described as the disciple who leans on Jesus' breast, the disciple who is deeply loved. Through Jesus, the Spirit had healed John and taught him how to love deeply and to be loved. But this did not mean that John avoided suffering in his life as an apostle.

In the last book of the Bible, Revelation, we learn that John has been exiled to the island of Patmos because of his preaching about Jesus: "I, John, your brother and companion in the suffering and kingdom and patient endurance that are ours in Jesus, was on the island of Patmos because of the word of God and the testimony of Jesus" (Revelation 1:9).

John uses three phrases that sum up the Christian life this side of Jesus' return: "the suffering and kingdom and patient endurance that are ours in Jesus" (Revelation 1:9). Being a Christian is wonderful: you are part of God's kingdom now, actively living under his reign now, adopted into his family and indwelt by his Spirit so that you know him personally. At that same time it involves suffering and thus patient endurance.

The book of Revelation encourages Christians under persecution with a view of heaven (*who* is really in charge) and a vision of the future to come (*why* it is so worthwhile to endure patiently). In every generation many Christians have tried to find in Revelation detailed clues to the end times, trying to connect what is going on today with what we find in Revelation. But this is not what Revelation does or why it was written. It is there to encourage us, to pull back the curtain so that we can peep into heaven and see who is really in control of history, how all God's promises will be fulfilled, and the future that God has promised is coming.

In his visions John sees an open door to heaven and is invited to come up through the door to see what is really going on (Revelation 4:1). John enters through the door to an astounding view and sound. He sees God on the throne as King over all, surrounded by the church of all ages, and an endless chorus of worship, singing hymns like

You are worthy, our Lord and God,
>
> to receive glory and honor and power,
>
for you created all things,
>
> and by your will they were created
>
> and have their being. (Revelation 4:11)

Again and again the pictures John receives are a powerful reminder that despite the persecution the Christians are undergoing, the living God is on the throne, his purposes are being worked out, and God will

triumph. Those who are persecuted are treasured by God and the time is coming when God will judge the earth and its peoples and eradicate his opponents and evil forever.

Whenever Handel's *Messiah* is performed, it is traditional to stand out of respect when the Hallelujah chorus is played. The Hallelujah chorus comes straight from the book of Revelation—namely, Revelation 11:15:

The kingdom of the world has become

the kingdom of our Lord and of his Messiah,

and he will reign for ever and ever.

The main theme of Jesus' teaching was the kingdom or reign of God. It arrived in Jesus but was still to come in all its fullness at the end of history, when Jesus comes again in power and might. It is this big picture of the future that Revelation fills out, again and again using the prophecies from the Old Testament, encouraging Christians to persevere and to live for God today.

From Revelation 11:15 we see that there is no hint of the world being destroyed and Christians going to heaven when Jesus returns. Instead the world becomes God's kingdom. Speaking of "going to heaven" is right in that heaven is especially where God lives, and he want us to be with him forever. But in terms of the end of our story, the Bible does not speak of going to heaven but of heaven coming down to earth. As John says,

Then I saw "a new heaven and a new earth," for the first heaven and the first earth had passed away, and there was no longer any sea. I saw the Holy City, the new Jerusalem, coming down out of heaven from God, prepared as a bride beautifully dressed for her husband. And I heard a loud voice from the throne saying, "Look! God's dwelling place is now among the people, and he will dwell with them. They will be his people, and God himself will be with them and be their God. 'He will wipe every tear from their eyes. There will be no more death' or mourning or crying or pain, for the old order of things has passed away." (Revelation 21:1-4)

The heaven and earth will be new, but not in the sense that the old is discarded. After all, it is God's good creation. But it is new in the sense that it is radically renewed. Evil is eradicated once and for all, and heaven—God's place—comes down to earth so that heaven and earth are now one. In the new Jerusalem the river of life is evocatively depicted as flowing from the throne of God with the tree of life on each side of the great river. The leaves of the tree, we are told, are for the healing of the nations (Revelation 22:2).

All God's people from all ages are gathered in the new creation. What *has* passed away are those things that make life so difficult, the causes of tears, death, and mourning.

And so, with act six of the great drama of the Bible, "The Return of the King: Redemption Completed," we come to the end. But it is, as one early Christian put it, an end that is no end but a whole new beginning—life in all its fullness, life as God intended it to be, human life, bodily life, life with God forever.

READINGS: Revelation 11:15-19 and 21:1-8

ACKNOWLEDGMENTS

PAIGE WOULD LIKE to thank Craig not only for his devoted work but also for his friendship, developed through the years of working together.

We are privileged to have worked with Br. Martin Erspamer, OSB, a monk of St. Meinrad Archabbey and a nationally renowned liturgical artist, on the magnificent illustrations he created for each chapter. These illustrations are not only beautiful, they're integral to the book. We are also grateful to Ethan McCarthy, our editor at IVP, for his support and valuable insight, as well as to editor Andy Le Peau for his thoughtful comments as the book developed. We are truly delighted to partner with IVP on the production of this book.

There are so many others to thank. Most importantly Paige's husband, Bob, whose thoughtful insight was the impetus for this book. A great deal of thanks goes to Joani, a gifted reader, who spent many hours reading, responding, and encouraging throughout the process. Paige would also like to thank the many family members and friends who have patiently listened, encouraged, and provided valuable feedback through the years. To them she owes a great debt of gratitude. To her parents who brought her up to know God through Jesus and for those bumpy roads in life that sent her in continual search of him, Paige is eternally grateful.

Finally, we are most grateful to you, our readers. No book is complete without you!

NOTES

1: Introduction

[1]There are many modern translations of the Bible available. Find one that you can understand. In this book we have used the New International Version (NIV). Other useful modern translations are the New Living Translation (NLT), The Good News Bible (GNB)/Good News Translation (GNT), the English Standard Version (ESV), the New Revised Standard Version (NRSV), etc.

[2]*Testament* means covenant or agreement. You will encounter the word *covenant* in several of the following chapters.

[3]Following Craig G. Bartholomew and Michael W. Goheen, *The True Story of the Whole World*; *The Drama of Scripture: Finding Our Place in the Biblical Story*, 2nd ed. (Grand Rapids, MI: Baker Academic, 2014).

2: Creation

[1]C. S. Lewis, *Miracles* (New York: Simon and Schuster, 1996), 140.

11: The Land

[1]This is a complex issue. An older book that remains useful on this topic is John Wenham, *The Goodness of God* (London: Inter-Varsity Press, 1974), especially chapter eight.

FURTHER READING AND RESOURCES

On our website, www.30minutebible.com or www.30minutebible.co.uk, you will find a variety of resources including discussion questions.

Other websites we recommend are

* www.biblesociety.org.uk/explore-the-bible/the-bible-course

* www.reframecourse.com

* https://bibleproject.com

If you want to study the Bible in greater depth, a good study Bible is invaluable. There are many out there. One we recommend is the *Biblical Theology Study Bible* published by Zondervan. Craig is one among many contributors.

The following publications go into greater depth about the big picture of the Bible's story and the believer's place in that drama.

* Craig G. Bartholomew and Michael W. Goheen, *The True Story of the Whole World: Finding Your Place in the Biblical Drama*, rev. ed. (Grand Rapids, MI: Brazos, 2020).

* Craig G. Bartholomew and Michael W. Goheen, *The Drama of Scripture: Finding Our Place in the Biblical Story*, 2nd ed. (Grand Rapids, MI: Baker Academic, 2014). A more advanced version of the above book.

* Bruce R. Ashford and Heath A. Thomas, *The Gospel of Our King: Bible, Worldview, and the Mission of Every Christian* (Grand Rapids, MI: Baker Academic, 2019).

* Michael W. Goheen and Jim Mullins, *The Symphony of Mission: Playing Your Part in God's Work in the World* (Grand Rapids, MI: Baker Academic, 2019).

For children:

* Sally Lloyd-Jones, *The Jesus Storybook Bible* (Grand Rapids, MI: Zondervan, 2012).